355.3 Goode, Stephen
GOO
The national defense
system

DATE			
MAY 2 '79			
MAR 11 '80			
MAY 30 '80			
SEP 28 '81			
OCT 23 '81			
4-14-82			
JAN 2 '84			

THE NATIONAL DEFENSE SYSTEM

THE NATIONAL DEFENSE SYSTEM

STEPHEN GOODE

Consulting Editor, Richard Darilek

Department of History
Herbert H. Lehman College
The City University of New York

Franklin Watts
New York | London | 1977

Cartoons courtesy of:

ROTHCO: (Ross) p. xii; (Pierotti) p. 6; (Juhl—
P.I.B., Copenhagen) p. 61; (Associated Newspapers, London) p. 63; (Graham–Arkansas
Gazette) pp. 67, 75, and SIDNEY HARRIS: pp. 50,
53, 73, 78, 88, 98.

Library of Congress Cataloging in Publication
Data

Goode, Stephen.
    The national defense system.

    Bibliography: p.
    Includes index.
    SUMMARY: Examines the military establish-
ment in the United States from its origin to the
present day and discusses the organization and
function of the Department of Defense.
    1.   United States—Armed Forces—Juvenile
literature.   2.   United States. Dept. of Defense
—Juvenile literature.   [1.   United States—
Armed Forces.   2.   United States. Department
of Defense]   I.   Title.
UA23.G73   355.3′0973   76–49039
ISBN 0–531–00398–1

For Diann McCormick

CONTENTS

This book was written in 1975, when the American defense establishment was celebrating its two hundredth birthday. On military bases throughout the country, parades and other events commemorated two centuries of American military history. Yet behind the celebration lay a great deal of uncertainty and soul searching. America had recently disengaged from a war that had divided the nation. Billions of dollars and thousands of lives had been lost on a long war that had finally ended when South Vietnam and Cambodia fell to Communist forces. Many Americans questioned the wisdom and efficiency of the military. They asked who was responsible. A desire spread throughout the country to limit and control the military in order to prevent any repetition of the disaster in Vietnam.

For their part, however, the people of the defense establishment argued that they were not to blame for the loss in Vietnam. To them it was obvious that the failure lay with the politicians—with the President and his advisers, and with many in Congress who had refused to give the military a free hand. There had been too many restrictions; politicians who had not understood the nature of warfare had dictated policy. No general or high-ranking official in the Defense Department felt it fair that the military be blamed for carrying out orders and policies that came from elsewhere.

Never before had the American military been so deeply called into question. Never before had so much resentment been displayed toward its power. The Bicentennial Year, then, seems a good time to survey the national defense establishment and come to some understanding of its workings and its problems. This book will do three things. After a brief sketch of the size, wealth, and influence of the American military, it will survey the history of the Armed Forces in the United States and its growth from a small, militia-type force into the most powerful military organization in the world. Next, this book will discuss the Department of Defense as it works today, its structure and makeup. There will be chapters on what the military does in the United States and on its military installations throughout the world. Finally, this book will describe the enormous political, economic, and other kinds of problems faced by the Defense Department while defending the United States against its enemies.

THE
NATIONAL
DEFENSE
SYSTEM

ROTHCO

"IS PEACE A NASTY WORD?"

CHAPTER ONE
The Department of Defense

The Department of Defense is the military wing of the United States government. It is responsible for defending the United States against all enemies. It satisfies that part of the Constitution that charges the federal government to "provide for the common Defence" of the American people. It is part of the executive branch of government and subject to the orders of the President, who is Commander in Chief of the Armed Forces. In the Defense Department are the Army, the Navy, and the Air Force. But there are also many civilian employees, who do research and help make military policy.

When the American military was first set up two hundred years ago, defense was not a complex problem. Enemies were far from our shores and transportation was slow. It took many weeks to travel from Europe. But in the twentieth century, vast improvements in transportation and technology have made defense an overriding concern. Weapons can now destroy whole cities in a matter of minutes. The Cold War—the prolonged conflict of ideas between the Soviet Union and the United States—has caused America to arm as never before. Defense has become big business. The military now permeates everyday life in this country.

When the Department of Defense was created, it was intended to be a center for top-level decision making. It was to be a relatively small branch of government, a center of clear thinking and realistic appraisal of military policies. It was not to get bogged down in the day-to-day administration in the Army, Navy, and Air Force. Yet in a short time the Department of Defense has become an agency of massive proportions. It is now the largest and most centralized bureaucracy in the non-Communist world, and by far the largest part of the American government. It has more than three and a half million employees, ranging from four-star generals to buck privates, from high-echelon civilians, such as the Secretary of Defense, to large numbers of specialists of all sorts: computer experts, astronomers, and social and political analysts. Indeed, there are few areas of knowledge neglected by the Department of Defense in its efforts to remain on top of world problems and provide defense. The department feels that in our complex modern world, no element or facet of life can be ignored in building up our national defense.

Defense Organization

The Department of Defense is intended to function as a well-oiled machine that can respond at moment's notice to any challenge an enemy of the United States might present. No other department of government is so centralized or has such a clear chain of command from low to high levels of authority. At the head of the Department is the Secretary of Defense. He is a civilian appointed by the President and serves as a member of the President's cabinet. His office is in the Pentagon. It is difficult to imagine the amount of power this man wields. He has direct access at any time to the President. But he also has direct contact with ships at sea and planes in the air. At any time he can telephone the Strategic Air Command in Omaha, Nebraska, or the North American Air Defense Command in Colorado Springs, Colorado. He also has tremendous control over the military budget, which gives him enormous power to distribute patronage and influence public opinion.

The Office of the Secretary of Defense includes the Secretary and his staff. Immediately under the Secretary is the Deputy Secretary, who serves as acting secretary when the Secretary of Defense is absent. Next in seniority is the Director of Defense Research and Engineering. That person serves as principal adviser and assistant in scientific and technical matters, an important post in the modern Department of Defense.

There are eight assistant secretaries of defense who hold responsibilities in eight fields. They deal with budgeting and fiscal affairs, health and environment, installations and logistics, intelligence, international security affairs, manpower and reserve affairs, public affairs, and systems analysis. There are other important officials on the Secretary's staff, who serve the Office of General Counsel, which gives legal advice, and who advise the Secretary on atomic energy, legislative affairs, and telecommunications. From looking at the various duties and responsibilities of the Secretary's staff, it is easy to see the wide range of interests of the modern military.

The body known as the Joint Chiefs of Staff consists of a chairman and the chiefs of the three services, the Army, Navy, and Air Force. The Commandant of the Marine Corps acts as a member when matters concerning the Marines are discussed. The members of the Joint Chiefs of Staff are each responsible to the Secretary of Defense. They act as the principal military advisers to the President, the Secretary of Defense, and the National Security Council—a group made up of the President, the Vice President, the Secretary of State, and the Secretary of Defense, whose collective duty it is to assess and appraise the objectives, commitments, and risks of the United States in relation to its actual and potential military power. The Joint Chiefs of Staff also direct the strategy—both individual and unified—of the different branches of the Armed Forces.

The military departments are the three services: the Army, the Navy, and the Air Force. Each service has its own civilian Secretary, who is appointed by the President (the Marine Corps is included under the Department of the Navy). These Secretaries work under the direction of the Secretary of Defense and the President. It is their responsibility to see that each service is prepared to carry out the policies developed by the President and his advisers. In our form of government, which guarantees civilian control of the military, the Secretaries are the last civilian link between the executive branch and the military departments.

The segment of the Pentagon known as the defense agencies has the responsibility of meeting specific defense requirements. The agencies include Defense Communications, Defense Contract Audit, Defense Intelligence, Defense Nuclear, Defense Security Assistance, and Defense Supply. Special care has been taken to ensure that the various offices and agencies of the Department of Defense have duties that do not overlap or conflict with one another.

Each individual service, of course, has its own organizational makeup. The Army, for instance, includes the Secretary of the Army, four assistant secretaries, and a Director of Civilian Defense, all of whom are civilians. The senior military official is the Chief of Staff of the Army. Under the Chief of Staff are the General Staff and the Special Staff. In the General Staff are such sections as the comptroller, personnel, intelligence, and logistics. In the Special Staff are units such as record keeping, finance, chaplains, military history, and others. Both the Navy and Air Force have similar components. To each staff, personnel of various ranks are assigned. The section of comptroller, for example, will include generals, colonels, majors, and so on.

The Department of Defense is not only the largest branch of the federal government, it is also the most expensive to run. Over the past thirty years, it has spent more than a trillion dollars on arms, weapons, soldiers, and improvements and changes of all sorts. It now spends well over a billion dollars every week (nearly 200 million per day), and consumes 10 percent of the nation's gross national product. Nearly twenty years ago, President Eisenhower characterized that enormous expenditure by showing what military money could buy if it were spent elsewhere: "The cost of one modern heavy bomber," he said, "is this: it is a modern brick school in more than 30 cities. It is two electric power plants, each serving a town of 60,000 population. It is two fine, fully equipped hospitals. It is some 50 miles of concrete highway."

Many Americans regret the large sums spent on defense, yet there are many others who argue that the country has had no alternative. The threat from the Soviet Union has been real, and the United States could not afford to be unprepared to meet that threat.

That brings us to an aspect of the Department of Defense that is even more impressive than its size or the amount of money it spends—its power. The Department of Defense, whose name is often abbreviated to DOD, controls the largest and strongest military force the world has ever seen. At the department's beck and call are enough nuclear bombs to destroy every square inch of the earth many times over.

Some of the newer weapons are truly terrifying. The atomic-powered Polaris submarine, for example, can stay underwater for long periods of time, move quickly, and deliver a nuclear warhead to any point in the world. Each of these submarines, which are about the size of a destroyer, carries 16 missiles, each missile measuring 28 feet in length. The missiles can be fired from the sub-

"THERE'S NONE LEFT FOR YOU, KID"

marine while it is submerged, at the rate of one a minute, and have a range of over 2,500 miles. Other, larger ground to ground missiles are equally amazing and can speedily deliver hydrogen warheads great distances with almost pinpoint accuracy. (In military language, pinpoint accuracy usually means within two miles of the target.) New tanks, faster planes, highly sophisticated radar, and other new weapons make the equipment used by the Armed Forces in World War II look primitive. But the military has no intention of limiting its resources to what's on hand, no matter how seemingly enormous its resources already are. Other, even more fantastic weapons are being worked on. Laser beams and weapons that can be fired from space will give the Armed Forces even greater punch. In the event of nuclear war, the Department of Defense hopes that it can inflict enough damage so that the enemy's war-making capacity is destroyed. Military men speak of 50 or 60 million enemy dead, with whole cities and industrial complexes wiped out. Such is the kind of power the military possesses and must control every day.

If the size, wealth, and power of the Defense Department are impressive, so too is the amount of influence it exerts on the lives of all Americans. A large portion of every tax dollar goes toward defense. One out of every ten men works for defense-related industry. Were the Department to stop its flow of money, millions of people would be out of work, with little prospect of finding work elsewhere. Millions of young men and women have served two or more years of their life in the military; many thousands have been killed or badly wounded while serving. No other branch of government asks so much of Americans or exerts so strong an influence.

But the Department of Defense controls our lives in subtler ways too. From an early fear of standing armies, the United States has become a nation led by those who see no possibility of disarmament. From a nation whose first President warned against "entangling alliances," and who felt it unwise for the country to get involved with foreign lands, numerous commitments have been established throughout the world. Those involvements have meant a major change in American life. General David Shoup, a war hero and a former Commandant of the Marine Corps, charges that "America has become a militaristic and aggressive nation," in violation of her nonmilitaristic traditions.

The Military-Industrial Complex

The problem was stated another way by President Eisenhower in his farewell address to the nation on January 17, 1961. Eisenhower had been a general in the Army before he entered civilian life—a highly respected Army man who had played an important part in World War II. In his farewell address as President, Eisenhower introduced a new phrase into the language. He said that Americans should beware of the "military-industrial complex." He pointed out that the United States was "the strongest, most influential and the most productive nation in the world." He said that it was natural for Americans to be very proud of that great productivity and strength, but he added that they should likewise be aware of new threats and challenges "new in kind and degree" that could undermine the American tradition of individual freedom and liberty.

Eisenhower pointed to the fact that until World War II, the United States had no permanent armaments industry. When war came, peacetime industries converted their factories. No major industry made its money from weapons and military equipment in time of peace. No longer, however, could we risk being without weapons and armaments. The threat to world peace has forced the United States to build a huge defense establishment and a permanent armaments industry. But this enormous expenditure, made to ward off outside threat, has itself threatened the economic, political, and spiritual values of the United States. What the citizens must guard against, Eisenhower concluded, was the acquisition of too much power and influence in industry and the military. They must not be led to believe that the most important things in American life were weaponry, missiles, and the preparation for war, for America had far more important values than these. Such warnings were all the more significant because they came from a man who had been a great general.

Later, the concept of the military-industrial complex was abbreviated to MIC, but under whatever name it was known, Eisenhower had been correct in seeing its potential strength and influence. Defense contracts have become the lifeblood of many of the largest and most important corporations in the United States. The wealth and well-being of a city, a congressional district, or even a whole state can depend on the amount of money the Department of Defense spends within its boundaries. For instance, when the Boeing Company, a manufacturer of aircraft, lost the contract for two important projects, the economy of the whole state of Washington, where the Boeing factories were situated, was affected. In 1963, military buying in the state had totaled well over a billion dollars. Only two years later, it had fallen to around $550 million. In Texas, California, and Georgia, the same was true. Defense spending was essential for a healthy and vigorous economy. Those areas have prospered in large part because of the many defense contracts they have received. Large, important corporations, such as Lockheed, General Dynamics, and others, could not have carried on business or made profits without defense contracts. Even industries whose primary business is not with the government, such as General Motors, Ford, and two major television networks, have received sizable government contracts that have helped expand business and increase profits.

Not only the business world, but also the world of education has profited from defense contracts. The Massachusetts Institute of Technology, Harvard, Johns Hopkins University, and the University of California have been able to carry on certain kinds of research only because the military budget provided the funds for needed sophisticated and expensive equipment. In March, 1966, Robert McNamara, then Secretary of Defense, told the Armed Services Committee of the House of Representatives that "the Department of Defense supports nearly half of all the academic research in the physical sciences and engineering now being done in American colleges and universities." Academics have been supported in researching areas other than science and engineering too. In 1956, the Institute for Defense Analysis (IDA) was set up by eight universities to handle studies in disarmament, civil defense, and various weapons systems. Its work included social and political studies as well as science reports. By the 1960s, universities had become so involved with the defense establishment that radical students demanded an end to the association between the military and institutions of higher learning.

But perhaps the most insidious way in which the military has changed American life is through our political system. Members of the House of Representatives and the Senate are anxious to have money spent in their respective districts. More money means more jobs and better salaries for voters. Contented voters mean re-election. The most extreme example of this practice was the case of the late Mendel Rivers, a congressman from South Carolina. Rivers was Chairman of the House Armed Forces Committee and wielded a great deal of power. He was considered a "superhawk," or one who strongly supported military expenditures. In his district, Charleston being its principal city, there came to be an Air Force base, an Army depot, a Naval shipyard, a Marine air station, the Parris Island Marine boot camp, two Naval hospitals, a Naval station, a Naval supply center, a Naval weapons station, a fleet ballistic-missile-submarine training center, a Polaris missile factory, an Avco Corporation plant (Avco does a great deal of business with the military), a Lockheed plant, and other defense-related factories and installations. The military payroll in the area is well over $2 billion a year. Rivers felt no reluctance in claiming responsibility for bringing over 90 percent of this business to his district.

Other senators and representatives have likewise profited from military largesse. The Armed Forces established bases and other installations in Georgia in order to win favor with the late Senator Richard Russell, Chairman of the Senate committee on the military. Texas and California have profited more than other states because of the ability and diligence of their representatives. On the other hand, a state like West Virginia, which gets little or no defense money, suffers from economic stagnation.

All this means that most representatives will bend over backward to please the military in order to obtain Defense Department spending. In a way, it is what President Eisenhower deplored when he warned of the power of the military-industrial complex. He feared that it might change and corrupt "the very structure of our society"—which seems to have become a reality when the military can pull political strings, buy the votes of elected representatives, and throw enormous sums of money around to influence opinion and attitude.

Several instances of undue influence and arm twisting that have undermined the democratic process of government have been exposed. In one case, a Republican congressman decided not to openly criticize the Secretary of Defense in a Democratic administration, even though he felt the Secretary needed criticism. The congressman feared that the Secretary might close down a military base in his district and cut down other federal funds that might be spent there. Free speech and open criticism, cornerstones of American democracy, had been thwarted. In another case, an admiral feared he might lose his job because he criticized Defense Department strategy before a Senate committee. Unlike the congressman, the admiral voiced his criticisms openly—and paid for it with his job. Time and again, writers, lawmakers, and others who have dared attack the military have found themselves subject to anonymous attacks and name calling. Their patriotism has been called into question, as though the only true patriots were the people of the Defense Department and their supporters.

The Pentagon

The center of Defense Department activity is the Pentagon, that famous five-sided building just across the Potomac River from Washington, D.C. The Pentagon has become a symbol of American military strength and influence. It is a huge building, almost a mile in circumference, and has seventeen miles of corridors and hallways. Those who work in the building are fond of telling the story of a paperboy who went in the front entrance when he was twelve years old, got lost, and did not find his way out until he was a lieutenant colonel. Over thirty thousand employees report to work every day in the one building alone. It is a city unto itself, with various business establishments, such as a bookstore, bank, post office, barbershop, department stores, laundry and dry cleaning stores, florist, bakery, pharmacy, candy stores, baggage lockers, Western Union telegraph office, optometrist, photo supply shop, newsstand, jewelry store, shoe repair shop, medical and dental clinics, as well as a gigantic parking lot. There are also lavish suites for generals and other high-ranking officials.

The history of the Pentagon itself parallels the history of the Department of Defense. The building was begun in 1941, when the defense establishment was changing and the United States was preparing for possible entry into World War II. At first meant to house only an elite corps of experts who would oversee planning, the Pentagon came to house the three branches of the armed services—the Army, Navy, and Air Force—for the first time under one roof. The original cost estimates predicted the Pentagon would require $35 million to build; its final cost was $83 million, the first of many cost underestimates that were to plague the Pentagon for the next thirty years.

From the beginning, the Pentagon had its critics. Some feared that such a large building implied that the military was planning to take over Washington and create its own empire. Others charged that it was unwise to house the most important elements of the American military under one roof, an easy target for enemy bombs. Still others claimed that the Pentagon would mar the beauty of Washington and of Arlington Cemetery. Military men, however, were convinced that new quarters were necessary, and that the United States should have a center of military power worthy of a powerful nation.

The Pentagon is the nerve center of the entire defense establishment. There the Army has its War Room and the Navy its Flag Plot area, where major decisions about war and peace are made. Here too is the command post of the Air Force. This command post has a worldwide communications network that keeps close tabs on every U.S. Air Force installation on earth. Every day constant checks are run on each piece of communications equipment to make sure it works. Continual drills keep communication workers alert; the military wants to know at all times what is happening. When an officer in the Pentagon pushes the Air Defense Command button, an officer at the Air Defense Command Post in Colorado Springs, Colorado, responds quickly. The same rapid response is obtained if the Pentagon calls London, England; Wiesbaden, Germany; or the Strategic Air Command Headquarters in Omaha, Nebraska.

We have now glimpsed some of the ways in which America's military organization obtained and uses its enormous power and influence to shape our lives. The Department of Defense is feared, hated, denounced, and envied the world over. To understand more fully the growth and development of this organization, it is necessary to go back over two centuries of American military history. By doing so we will find out what attitudes Americans have held toward the Armed Forces, as well as come to understand the changes that have taken place in the military itself over the years. And only then can we evaluate General Shoup's accusation that America has become a militaristic society, a nation interested only in war and power.

Two characteristics dominated the early American attitude toward defense. The first was confidence in the militia system, an army of citizens who could be called at a moment's notice to rise up and defend their homes and property. The second was a deep-seated belief that a standing army was a dangerous and evil thing, and, for the sake of freedom and liberty, to be avoided at all costs. To understand the origin of that double-edged attitude is to understand an important part of early American history; both traditions were peculiarly American, and both took a long time to die out.

The Militia Ideal

The militia system was a logical outcome of the colonial experience. On the frontier, everyone had to be concerned with defense. Boys were trained from an early age to use a rifle. They hunted squirrels, turkeys, and raccoons to add to the family food supply, and in the process trained themselves for warfare. Wars at that time were primarily directed against the native Americans, the Indians. From time to time, Dutch, French, or Spanish sailing vessels would threaten American towns, but the Indians were always there, and always had to be reckoned with.

The colonists learned very early that the Indians did not fight by standards of European warfare. They fought on their own territory, not on a formal battlefield. The fighting forces that developed in the early colonies therefore relied on individual people of the locality. Distances were simply too great and transportation too poor to be able to depend on a centralized military force. The settlers had to be ready at a moment's notice to take up arms for attack or defense. When an incident occurred, the men would rush to arms and remain armed until the disturbance was over. Then they would disband and return to their farming.

Women took part too. Mrs. Experience Bogarth, for example, defended her family and several neighbor families who had taken refuge in her home. The men were seriously injured and could not fight. Mrs. Bogarth axed to death three attackers. She chopped open the heads of two victims, and disemboweled the third.

In Massachusetts after 1633, each man was required to have a musket, a cartridge belt, a sword, two pounds of powder, and ten pounds of bullets. Further laws in Massachusetts and in the other colonies developed the militia system more precisely. The colonial militia was a military organization made up of citizen soldiers. Every able-bodied man was armed, and each town had its own company. The companies held regular training sessions and inspections of arms, so that the men would be prepared for attack. Such a system was very different from the practice in Europe, where kings and governments never placed any weapons in the hands of the people for fear that the people would rise up and overthrow them.

As a result of so much hunting and fighting, the rifle in America quickly developed into a far more efficient instrument than the European rifle. By the time of the American Revolution, in fact, the reputation of the American rifle and the frontier marksman was so widespread that many Englishmen were afraid of war in America. General Washington took advantage of that fear and encouraged his men to wear frontier marksmen's outfits even if they were not frontier marksmen. According to Washington, "the Hunting shirts, with long Breeches made of the same cloth . . . is a dress justly supposed to carry no small terror to the enemy, who think every such person a complete Marksman."

A Standing Army

The second part of the attitude of the colonists toward the military—the fear of a standing army—developed from experiences in Europe. Many colonists had been driven to America in the first place because they held opinions not popular in their home countries. They knew from experience that a state could derive —and misuse—a great deal of power from a standing army. Such an army could be used to put down dissent and impose the will of those in power on those who happened not to be in power. A standing army would go looking for a war to fight. A standing army might force a man to leave home and travel long distances to fight in battles he did not understand. For the colonists, it was important to be left alone and allowed to provide for their own defense, in their own way.

That feeling was so strong, in fact, that one American colony would seldom, if ever, send soldiers or financial aid to another colony. Americans were likewise reluctant to serve in the British army stationed in America. The British had to protect its American garrison with professional soldiers brought from Europe. It is important to remember that one of the causes of the Revolution was the resentment brought on when Americans were required to house and support British troops. They were so resentful, in fact, that later, they included a statement in the Bill of Rights of the Constitution forbidding the quartering of soldiers in private houses without the consent of the owner.

Even the outbreak of the War for Independence did not change American attitudes toward war. Although Americans were fighting for a cause, General Washington found it difficult to obtain recruits for a national army. Most men wanted to serve in their local militia so that they could remain close to their homes. Even those who enlisted in the army did so for only a short time and were anxious to return home once their few months of service were completed. Desertions were commonplace; even in the heat of battle, American soldiers fled before the professional British soldiers. At the famous battle of Guilford Court House, for example, the flight of the militia into the woods gave victory to the British, even though the Americans outnumbered them by more than three to two. A European observer of the time noted that there was no discipline in the American army and that the Americans were "impatient under all kinds of superiority and authority." He did not believe that a successful army could be formed out of such men.

As the Revolutionary War drew to a close, the Continental Congress asked General Washington what he felt should happen once peace came. Washington responded with his "Sentiments on a Peace Establishment," in which he expressed his belief that the new nation would need a small standing army to deal with the Indians. In case of foreign invasion, he felt that army could be expanded by the addition of militia units. Washington also recommended that the various state militias be organized into a single national militia. In that way, he argued, the militia could be organized and equipped. He also saw the need for the development of war-related industries to provide weapons and ammunition and the creation of a national arsenal. Finally, he recommended that Congress establish a school to train officers for the small army.

But the Congress chose to ignore his recommendations. At the end of the war, most of the army was disbanded, except for eighty men to guard supplies at Fort Pitt and at West Point. The general feeling was against a defense establishment. John Adams, later to be the second President of the United States, saw virtue only in a militia. From a standing army he expected "corruption and violence," which would destroy the new republic. Thomas Jefferson, soon to be the third President, held similar views. In a letter to James Madison, he said that he wanted in the Constitution protection from standing armies. Later Jefferson likewise wrote, "I am for relying, for internal defense, on our militia solely, till actual invasion, and for such a naval force only as may protect our coasts and harbors from such depredations as we have experienced; and not for a standing army in time of peace, which may overawe the public sentiment; nor for a navy, which, by its own expenses and the eternal wars in which it will implicate us, will grind us with public burthens, and sink us under them."

Constitutional Statements

When the Constitution was framed, it reflected the opinions of these men. Control of the military was placed firmly in the hands of civilians. The President, an elected official, was to be Commander in Chief. Congress, filled with elected delegates from every state and district, was to have the power to declare war and control the military budget. The Bill of Rights, the first ten amendments to the Constitution, guaranteed the rights the colonists had fought for such as "a well regulated Militia, being necessary to the security of a free State, the right of the people to keep and bear Arms, shall not be infringed." The Constitution made no specific recommendation concerning a standing army. It was more anxious to determine the definite freedoms and liberties of the individual and the responsibilities of the three branches of government. The nature of the American military was left for others to work out.

Thus when George Washington became the first President under the new Constitution, one of the problems he faced was what to do about the military. He told his Secretary of War, Henry Knox, to design legislation for Congress based on his "Sentiments on a Peace Establishment," with a small standing army, an armaments industry, and a college to train officers. But in the Militia Act of 1792, Congress rejected the idea of a centrally organized militia. As Senator William Maclay of Pennsylvania said in opposition to the plan, "Give Knox his army and he will soon have a war on hand." The new congress did not see the military as providing defense against aggression and war. On the contrary, it believed the standing army was an invitation for war and would inevitably get the country involved in war. What the Congress provided was a very small army of eight hundred forty officers and men, a force that would offer no threat to the government or society.

The problem of a navy faced similar controversy. From the beginning, America had depended on ships and shipping for trade and commerce; the sea was very much a part of American life. During the Revolution, a navy had been created to defend the nation's ports and break the blockades imposed by the British, and in the beginning of the war, the Continental Navy of about sixty ships had made a good showing. Eventually, however, it had become necessary to get aid from the French, and it was the French fleet, in fact, that had added the necessary punch to defeat the British. Yet under the Constitution, Congress decided that a navy was not necessary. Even more than an army, it was felt, a navy would get America involved in foreign wars. Anything that might bring the new nation into conflict with Europe was avoided like the Plague.

Before long, however, reality intervened and forced the Americans to change their minds about their armed forces. Washington had persuaded Congress that a small standing army was necessary to fight the Indians, and during the 1790s, new outbreaks of Indian fighting brought about an enlargement of that force. It was the same with the navy. In 1794, pirate ships from the Barbary States along the northern coast of Africa attacked American ships engaged in commerce. Congress was forced to authorize the building of six frigates and to establish a Navy Department. That department was kept separate from the Department of War until the National Security Act of 1947 united the various branches of the Armed Forces.

The Development of the Army

Between 1789 and the War of 1812, the size of the Army rose and fell according to the Indian situation. For the most part, the United States still relied on the militia.

It was the War of 1812, however, that first demonstrated the folly of relying on the militia for defense during a genuine national emergency. In that war, a rapidly expanded army of 60,000 had to bear the brunt of fighting against a larger force of British, Canadians, and Indians. The state militias proved inadequate to meet the challenge. At Bladensburg, Maryland, a force of 6,500 militiamen defending the capital at Washington fled in terror after one volley from a force of only 1,500 Englishmen. The city of Washington was taken by the enemy and burned. After the war, the standing army was set at 10,000, the largest it had ever been in time of peace. It fluctuated between 6,000 and 12,000 until the Mexican War (1846–48), having reached its peak in the 1830s during the Seminole War in Florida.

During the Mexican War, the United States ceased to rely on the militia for war purposes, and it became customary to depend on volunteers for a national army. Indeed, soon after the outbreak of the war, the army was rapidly increased to 30,000 men, and soon 60,000 more volunteers were added. Only 12,000 militiamen were called up, who remained on active duty only three months and saw no action in Mexico. The relative ease with which the army defeated the Mexicans and occupied Mexico City contributed to its reputation and prestige. By that time, both the Army and Navy had academies to train officers and establish military tradition. The U.S. Military Academy had been established in 1802 at West Point, New York. The Naval Academy, founded in 1845, was at Annapolis, Maryland.

The Civil War again underlined the inadequacies of the traditional militia system. At the beginning of the war, 75,000 militiamen were called up for the standard three-month enlistment. The overwhelming source of military strength, however, came from those who volunteered for the regular army. Nearly 3 million men volunteered their services during that war, with half that number seeing action at any one time.

The Civil War was the first great war of America's history, and one of its bloodiest. It gave Americans the first taste of how bitter and ugly war could be. There was the usual reaction after the war: the standing army was reduced to 54,000 and then to 25,000. Congress provided little money for military matters, with the result that the Army was low paid and ill equipped. Most soldiers saw action in the West, against the Indians. Those were the days of the cavalry and the Indian attacks on the forts of the Arizona and Montana territories. It was also the time of Custer's Last Stand at Little Bighorn.

The United States Navy

The Navy, on the other hand, underwent expansion during the nineteenth century. Gone were the days when Congress feared the entanglement with foreign nations that a navy might bring. The War of 1812 added to the prestige of American sea power. In spite of its small size, the Navy gained impressive victories over the much larger British fleet. The size of the British fleet had much to do with Congress's decision to expand the American navy—the war itself had grown out of the arrogant display of power by the British. British ships stopped American ships and forced American sailors to serve in the British navy, a practice known as impressment. During the war, the British blockade was effective and enabled the British to attack Baltimore, New Orleans, and various other ports. Americans thus experienced firsthand the dangers a small navy could bring.

After the War of 1812, the Navy began to play a much larger role in American life. It began to appear in port cities throughout the world, making the American presence felt. It explored and surveyed new territory. It opened up Japan to Western trade and aided commerce elsewhere in the Near and Far East. It assisted on scientific expeditions and studies, and it contributed greatly toward the suppression of piracy and the slave trade. During the Mexican War, the Navy occupied California, and ran the government. During the Civil War, it blockaded southern ports, slowing down southern trade and preventing the transportation of war supplies to the South. After the war, however, the Navy was neglected for many years, and allowed to fall behind the pace of development kept by the navies of other countries.

A century after the founding of the nation, the militia ideal had begun to disappear, but no one yet thought in terms of a large standing army. No congressman or President envisioned America as a great military power. Indeed, the destruction and slaughter of the Civil War had turned American minds away from war for a while. The early American fear of the military and a standing army was still strong. All the same, new forces were at work, forces that saw the United States as a world power, with colonies and overseas possessions. Such new attitudes were changing people's minds about the role the young country should play in the world, and along with that change in attitude, came a reappraisal of the American military.

American attitudes toward foreign entanglements and military power again began to change in the 1890s. The frontier was gone, and the country had expanded about as far as it could within continental boundaries. The great nations of the world—Britain, France, Germany, and others—had colonial empires that brought them wealth and fame. A hundred years earlier, President Washington had warned against involvement with the affairs of Europe or other lands. He thought that the United States should pursue a policy of isolation, steering clear "of permanent alliances, with any portion of the foreign world." Now, however, many in the United States argued that their country should join the quest for empire. They saw the United States as a great power that should make its influence felt in the world. Parts of Asia were still free for the asking. There were islands in the Pacific that could act as ports for U.S. ships trading with the Far East. To a nation that had just begun to realize its enormous wealth and power, those were tempting goals indeed.

Mahan's *Sea Power*

One of the most prominent early supporters of expansion was Captain Alfred Thayer Mahan. In 1890, Mahan published *The Influence of Sea Power Upon History 1660–1783.* It was a book that was to have a very large influence on American military development and to gain fame for its author. It was Mahan's belief that "no nation, certainly no great nation, should henceforth maintain a policy of isolation." Mahan stated simply that "whether they will or no, Americans must now begin to look outward."

Captain Mahan was primarily concerned with naval power, for he felt that only the nation that commanded the seas was in a position of real power. Such a nation could carry on trade wherever it wanted, and its ships would not be threatened or attacked by those of other nations. American industry needed new lands in which to sell its goods. The laws of economics were simple: if economic expansion and growth were to continue, the United States would have to find foreign markets. It would have to possess or at least control ports throughout the world where American ships could refuel and be repaired.

The U.S. Navy could therefore be of use in aiding American commerce. Its role would be more than the defense of the nation; the new Navy would be the core of a prosperous, powerful America. Mahan urged the building of a canal across the Isthmus of Panama. He advocated U.S. supremacy in the Caribbean. He urged that Americans take control of Hawaii and Samoa. The United States could not become an imperialist power, he wrote in 1894, unless it abandoned its traditional attitudes toward war and the military. The nation would have to "cast aside the policy of isolation which befitted her infancy" and assume commitments throughout the world. This was the nation's "inevitable task, and appointed lot in the work of upholding the common interests of civilization."

Mahan found support for his doctrines in two important political leaders. Senator Henry Cabot Lodge of Massachusetts echoed his sentiments on the Senate floor. "It is the seapower that is essential to the greatness of every great people," said Lodge. He further asked for the annexation of Cuba and the growth of American power in the world. Theodore Roosevelt, who was Civil Service Commissioner at the time, likewise accepted Mahan's doctrines. He was later to carry them into effect as Secretary of the Navy under President McKinley, and then in his own right as President. Roosevelt called for a large and strong navy. "Peace is a goddess only when she comes girt with a sword on her thigh," he said, and on another occasion he advised the United States "to speak softly and carry a big stick." Mahan, Lodge, and Roosevelt spoke for a growing number of Americans. The *Washington Post* summed up the new feeling succinctly: "A new consciousness seems to have come upon us—the consciousness of strength—and with it a new appetite, the yearning to show our strength."

The Spanish-American War, fought over Cuba and the Philippines, offered an early test of the new imperialist fervor. When a U.S. ship, the *Maine*, was blown up in Havana harbor under mysterious circumstances, war fever and desire for vengeance struck the nation. Volunteers joined the Army in large numbers. In a short time, 216,029 men were in uniform. The war with Spain went quickly. The old Empire crumbled easily, and on its ruins the new American empire and military reputation was built. Roosevelt's charge up Kettle Hill (not San Juan Hill, as is often stated) in Cuba with his Rough Riders and Dewey at Manila in the Philippines offered instances of heroism and military action that were discussed for many years. The United States gained Puerto Rico, Cuba, and the Philippines, as well as islands in the Pacific.

Yet all was not well. The rapid expansion of the Army at the beginning of the war had been chaotic and difficult. Adequate transportation had not been available. There were no summer uniforms for the men to wear, nor were there weapons enough to arm all the volunteers. Food was poor, and no precautions were taken against sickness. For every man killed in battle, fourteen died of disease. The War Department was revealed to all as inefficient and backward. Administration and organization drastically needed reform; the whole operation of the military needed review. To accomplish such reorganization, McKinley appointed Elihu Root as his new Secretary of War. Root has come to be regarded as one of the greatest men ever to hold that office, for he succeeded in revamping not only the War Department itself, but also United States military policy. Under him, the military first began to take on the character it has today.

Reorganization of the Army and Navy

Secretary Root had been a corporation lawyer with no military background when he became a member of McKinley's cabinet. In looking for a model upon which to base his reforms, he chose the most powerful and respected army of the day, the German army. The result was the Army Reorganization of 1903. Its most important innovation was the creation of a general staff system, headed by a Chief of Staff. This move helped to centralize and give order to the War Department. Under this act, the administrative tools of the department were put into the hands of one person, the Chief of Staff, who became the military adviser to the Secretary of War and the President. The Secretary of War, on the other hand, had both the power to remove the Chief of Staff and control over the military budget. In that way, complete civilian control over the military was retained. At the end of the Spanish-American War, the Army was maintained at 100,000 men, partly in order to put down nationalist rebels in the Philippines who resented American occupation as much as they had resented Spanish rule.

In keeping with Mahan's doctrines, the Navy was expanded. It won easy victories during the Spanish-American War. When Roosevelt became President upon the assassination of McKinley in 1900, he used his power to carry out Mahan's ideas even more fully. In 1907–08, he sent the new and impressive U.S. fleet around the world to put in at various ports, and demonstrate American power and prestige. But genuine administrative reform did not come to the Navy as it had to the Army. There was no Elihu Root to effect such reform. Further, jealousies among the various admirals made change difficult. The few radical reformers in the Navy were unable to make their opinions felt.

Another reform reflected the new character of the military in the United States. In 1916, the Militia Act of 1792 was abolished. The militia system had proved inadequate in almost every war since the Revolution, but it had been preserved as part of the national heritage. To replace the old system, the National Guard was set up. The Guard is under federal supervision, with component units in every state. In peacetime, it is commanded by the state governments, but can be called into national service by the orders of the President. Guard units are equipped by the federal government, and required to be similarly organized in every state. The Army Reserve was likewise created at this time. It grew out of the tradition of volunteers who had fed the regular army in the Mexican War and the Civil War. Since its inception, it has acted as a reservoir for trained commissioned and noncommissioned officers. Thus by 1916, the nation had finally adopted the policies outlined by General Washington in his "Sentiments on a Peace Establishment."

When the United States entered World War I in 1917, many historians believe that it was better prepared for war than at any other time in its history. Such preparedness was due in large part to the reforms that Root had begun fifteen years earlier, but also to the experience the military had gained since the beginning of the century. The Army had gotten background and training in the Philippines, where its presence was necessary to keep order. It had likewise acquired experience during the Mexican incident of 1916, when President Woodrow Wilson ordered U.S. forces under General Pershing to enter Mexico and capture Pancho Villa, a Mexican rebel leader who had raided several American towns. Pershing failed to capture Villa, but the incident had required a rapid mobilization of the regular army and 65,000 National Guardsmen, which was carried off efficiently.

When the United States entered the World War, the conflict was already three years old and stalemated. Neither side seemed capable of winning. In a short time, the United States gave the Allies the final push needed. During the year and a half it was involved in the war, the United States called up 4 million soldiers. Most of these men were brought into the Army by the Selective Service Act of 1917, known as "the draft." The draft obliged men to serve two years in the Army; those who refused were punished by imprisonment. Nearly 25 million men between the ages of 18 and 45 were registered under the Act. Of these, 2,180,296 were inducted into the Army. World War I saw the creation of a new division of the Armed Forces called the Aeronautical Division of the Signal Corps of the Army. It was our earliest air force. When the United States entered the war, the Aeronautical Division had a little over 100 men, and only 103 airplanes, not one of which was ready for combat. When the war ended, the Division had 195,000 men and 740 airplanes. But only a few visionaries saw the Air Force as the wave of the future.

The Navy played a less significant role than the Army in World War I, but it too proved important. A shipbuilding program begun in 1916 helped the Navy prepare for entry in the war, and by 1918, it had grown to eight times its prewar size. Not only did ships transport the United States Army to Europe, they also laid mines to destroy German submarines. U.S. ships did not participate in any great sea battles, but the war nevertheless could not have been won without them.

When peace came in November, 1918, a new wave of isolationism spread across the United States, comparable to the isolationism experienced after the Mexican and Civil wars, when Americans had grown weary of war and standing armies. Not all Americans had wholeheartedly supported the entry of the United States into a "European war." Even Senator Lodge, who had supported Mahan's theories, shied away from foreign entanglements and opposed any further commitments abroad. The wartime army of 4 million was shrunk to 125,000. No other victorious power had so small a military force. In Congress, many thought that American blood should never again be spilt to solve problems in foreign lands.

The Navy too suffered neglect. The Washington Treaty of 1922 and the London Naval Treaty of 1930 limited the number of ships allowed to navies throughout the world. At the time, these treaties were hailed as great victories for peace. Later, some Americans would wonder if the country had been unduly quick to disarm and whether a larger navy would have helped prevent World War II.

The height of antiwar feeling was reached in 1928 with the so-called Kellogg-Briand Pact. Frank B. Kellogg, the U.S. Secretary of State, and Aristide Briand, the French foreign minister, drew up an agreement that was signed by sixty-five nations, including the United States and the Soviet Union. In that agreement, the nations announced that they condemned war as an instrument of national policy. So low had the American military fallen, that by 1938, the year before World War II began in Europe, the Chief of Naval Operations confessed that the Navy was "approaching inferiority in defensive power." The Army Chief of Staff added that the Army suffered from "marked inferiority in strength."

Indeed, we of today must look back on the U.S. Army of only forty years ago with some amazement. The nation is so accustomed to a huge military that it seems as if things must have always been as they are now. In 1935, the U.S. Army was the sixteenth largest army in the world. Czechoslovakia, Turkey, Spain, Rumania, Poland, and Yugoslavia all had larger armies. Pay was low (a private received only $17.85 a month), and the military budget was scanty (the Army of the thirties cost roughly one fourth of one percent of the cost of today's military establishment). Many officers found their lives boring. Dwight D. Eisenhower, at the time a major and aide to Douglas MacArthur, the Army Chief of Staff, nearly resigned his commission because he found himself stagnating. James Gavin, then a lieutenant stationed in the Philippines and later a general as well as an outspoken critic of U.S. policy in Vietnam, has given us a picture of what it meant to be in the Army of that time. "The drill days were rather short and there was an abundance of time for extracurricular activities. I should have spent more time on my books, but tennis, golf and riding offered too much competition." It was a time when most Americans felt little concern for military matters. A Gallup poll taken in January, 1937, showed that 85 percent of the country felt there would be no war. Even as late as May, 1939, 68 percent still believed there would be no war.

But for some time, events had seemed to indicate otherwise. Germany had rearmed and was under the leadership of Adolf Hitler, a fanatic with dreams of conquering Europe and perhaps the world. Italy was fascist and aggressive. In the Far East, Japan had shown its strong imperialist tendencies and its interest in conquering China and much of Asia. Around the world, peace was threatened. But in spite of these events, as late as 1938 the War Plans Division of the Army had only two plans for mobilization in case of war. Plan Red was for a war against Great Britain, which was highly unlikely. Plan Red and Orange was for an attack by a coalition of Great Britain and Japan.

Early in 1938, however, President Franklin D. Roosevelt had

grown concerned about the condition of the military. Reports from Europe troubled him, and he wrote to Edward Taylor, a member of the House of Representatives and Chairman of the House Appropriations Committee, which helped plan the national budget. "World events have caused me growing concern," the President wrote. "In the world as a whole, many nations are not only continuing but enlarging their armament programs. . . . Facts are facts and the United States must face them." The result of such concern was that Roosevelt increased his budget for the Navy to more than it had been any year since 1920. Soon he developed his plans into the Naval Expansion Act. This act called for a "two-ocean navy" so that America could protect its interests in both the Atlantic and the Pacific.

Nor was the Army to be neglected. In June, 1938, Congress voted a record military budget for peacetime—over a billion dollars. It included many important features: the largest peacetime appropriation ever provided for Army supplies and equipment, money for new antiaircraft guns, for semiautomatic rifles and improved artillery. An enlargement of the fleet and an increase in the number of planes was likewise ordered. Indeed, President Roosevelt, against the advice of many of his staff, had concluded that air power was of primary importance. Reports had told him of the terrible power of the German army and air force, and he wanted the United States to be ready to meet them. He knew, for instance, that the United States had only 1,700 combat-ready planes, while the Germans had 10,000. Furthermore, Germany had the capacity to turn out 12,000 planes a year, far more than the United States could produce.

In convincing the war-reluctant nation that his programs were necessary, Roosevelt moved slowly. He knew well the fear and mistrust that military spending and expansion aroused in the minds of the public. He also knew the strong sentiment in Congress for isolationism. Many important senators and representatives were staunchly antiwar. They believed in the old American tradition of distrusting standing armies. Yet the President stood convinced of the necessity for rearmament and preparedness. Thus the administration called military spending "economic pump priming." The country was in the midst of a depression, the most severe it had ever known. Jobs were needed for millions of men and women. The fact that 85 percent of the money poured into Naval ship construction actually went into the pockets of wage earners made the expenditure more acceptable to many in Congress and elsewhere. It was difficult to oppose a policy that led to both improvement in national defense and more jobs for Americans.

Another move that helped put the nation more firmly on a wartime footing was the Selective Service Act of 1940. The draft had come to an end after World War I; thus the act of 1940 was the first peacetime conscription that the United States had ever experienced. For some time, a few Army and Navy junior officers had been studying the feasibility of a new selective service system. They had been ordered to keep their investigation secret so that opponents of the military could not say that the United States was preparing for war. These young officers became overwhelmingly convinced that the United States should be better prepared for war. They were rewarded when the new act passed that provided for a steady flow of men into the Armed Forces and made possible a quick call-up of large numbers of men in case of war. It was at that time too that the planning for the Pentagon to house the improved and expanded military was begun.

World War II

The war came on December 7, 1941, when Japan attacked the American base at Pearl Harbor, in Hawaii. Within two hours, 8 battleships, 3 light cruisers, 188 airplanes, and 4 important shore installations were destroyed or badly damaged. American dead numbered 2,403. The American forces at Pearl Harbor responded to the attack with little effect. News of the attack did not reach the Navy Department until six hours after it had happened. In a few days, the United States was at war with Japan, Germany, and Italy. Isolationism was over. The country had again entered the international arena. In a speech delivered on December 9, 1941, the President told the American people, "We are in the war, we are all in it—every single man, woman, and child is a partner in the most tremendous undertaking of our American history." The President himself assumed his role of Commander in Chief, and became one of the most active Presidents ever, in a war cause.

World War II forced the United States into deeper involvement than any other war in its history. Eight million men and women were in uniform at the height of the war. Many more worked long hours in war industries at home. Women took on a lion's share of the work. For the first time, the government spent large sums of money on research. Lucrative incentives were given to private industry to increase their production. Since the frequent changes in design and planning made it difficult to estimate how much a new military item would cost, the government announced the "cost plus a fixed fee" contract. Under the terms of this contract, the government agreed to meet all the expenses incurred by the manufacturer, and in addition pay a fixed fee, so that profit was guaranteed. Thus the government took all the risks involved in production, and private industry assumed the profits—profits which rose substantially in the next few years.

Private research institutions were likewise heavily subsidized for the first time. In 1930, only $130 million was spent on scientific research, but after the war began, the Massachusetts Institute of Technology alone received $116 million, and the Office of Scientific Research and Development distributed many hundreds of millions more. The money was not ill spent, for out of the war came hundreds of new and significant discoveries: radar, jet propulsion, rockets, for example, and, of course, the atomic bomb. The war even contributed to the development of DDT and other insecticides, penicillin, and new techniques for packaging blood and blood substitutes.

Americans were happy to see the end of World War II. It had been a long, hard war and had taken the lives of 291,557 Americans and left 670,846 wounded. Perhaps no war in American history had inspired so many, for it had been fought to rid the world of the evils of fascism and Nazism. Most Americans held the naive belief that the war had settled world problems, at least for a while, and began to act as if it had. Once again the desire for disarmament and isolation seized the country. From the wartime high of 8 million, the number of men in uniform dropped to 3 million in January, 1946. Two years later, it had fallen to 554,000. Moreover, those who had gained experience in World War II were the first to go, so that the new Army was made up of raw recruits. The Navy and the Air Force were likewise demobilized and shrunk.

But before long, a new threat to world peace and security arose. The Soviet Union, an ally in World War II, had become an enemy. Agreements between the American and Soviet governments were repeatedly violated. One by one, the nations of Eastern Europe were occupied by Soviet forces: Czechoslovakia, Rumania, Bulgaria, Hungary, Yugoslavia, and Poland. The Russians remained in East Germany and threatened to cut off access to East Berlin, the Soviet sector of the city. Soon wars between Communist insurgents and established governments were breaking out all over the world. In Greece and Iran, but most importantly in China, the Communists grew strong. On October 1, 1949, Mao Tse-tung established a Communist regime on mainland China. America's ally, Chiang Kai-shek, was driven to the small island of Taiwan. To many, it was frightening that in a short time, one out of every three people on earth had become subject to Communist rule.

The final straw came when North Korean Communist forces invaded South Korea in 1950. Under the auspices of the United Nations, American forces were drawn into the conflict. General Douglas MacArthur, the U.S. military governor of occupied Japan, was asked to become commander of a combined U.N. force of American, British, French, Dutch, Australian, Turkish, and Philippine troops. After a few initial defeats, the troops were reinforced by experienced U.S. soldiers and by stores of U.S. arms and ammunition. Soon MacArthur and his troops had driven the North Koreans deep into their own territory. But just then, the war took on a new complexion.

Chinese Communist forces—numbering more than 200,000—entered the war on the side of North Korea. MacArthur was driven back into South Korea. The capital of South Korea fell to the Communists for the second time in the war. After a long and hard struggle, the U.N. troops restored the capital and regained territory. But a bitter fight broke out between President Harry Truman and General MacArthur. Truman wanted to end the war; General MacArthur wanted to prolong it by bombing Communist China. The conflict ended when the President dismissed MacArthur. The war itself ended some time later, with a compromise between North and South Korea and their allies.

Reorganization of Defense

The Communist threat in Europe and Asia precipitated a demand for change and reorganization in the defense establishment. The first winds of change came in 1947 and 1949, when Congress passed two important bills relating to the Armed Forces. The first, the National Security Act of 1947, created the National Military Establishment, consisting of three military departments and headed by the Secretary of Defense. The first was the Department of the Army, which replaced the old Department of War, which had been in existence since the time of President Washington. The second was the Air Force, which was separated from the Army, in which it had been included since before World War I. The third military department was the Navy. The new Secretary of Defense became a member of the President's cabinet, along with each of the three Secretaries of the military departments. It was the duty of the Secretary of Defense to formulate general military policy. The National Security Act of 1947 also formally created the Joint Chiefs of Staff, and provided that the Joint Chiefs be assisted by a Joint Staff. The Joint Chiefs and their staff would be professional military personnel who could advise and assist the Secretary of Defense and the President. Congress felt that the National Security Act of 1947 would create a better organized and more efficient military.

In 1949, that act was modified by the National Security Act of 1949. The new act created the Department of Defense to replace the National Military Establishment. The Secretary of Defense was given greater power over the department and became the only member of the President's cabinet to represent the military. The Secretaries of the Army, Navy, and Air Force were demoted from the cabinet and made responsible to the Secretary of Defense. This later act, then, further centralized the authority of the department. Two more acts of Congress, in 1953 and 1958, added to the Secretary's power, the purpose of the legislation being to undermine the independence of the three branches of the Armed Forces and limit rivalry. A constant problem was the jealousy with which the Navy guarded its "rights" against encroachment by the Army or Air Force—each service felt threatened by the power or expansion of the other's. It was hoped that a strong Secretary of Defense could control such rivalry.

The United States military had come a long way since the beginning of the century. Gone were the traditions that had been so firmly ingrained in the minds of the original colonists. The militia concept died out because it could not provide the power needed for a major national emergency. Isolationism had disappeared because an increase in power and foreign interests had forced the country to become involved throughout the world. Opposition to a standing army had dissolved because most Americans thought that a strong, well-armed, and well-prepared nation was essential for preventing what was perceived as Communist aggression all over the world. However, in the next thirty years, military tradition would again be changed in the United States, changed to meet the more modern kinds of crises the world was beginning to face.

The Korean War taught America two difficult lessons. First, it emphasized the need for preparedness and a large military establishment. When the war began, rearmament was sped up and defense spending greatly increased. The modern, massive American war machine dates from that time. But second, the Korean War presented the United States with an issue its leaders had never faced before: just how much and where to limit the necessarily limited war, a war whose goal was something less than total victory. Never before in American history had the conflict between the military and the civilian government been so severe. General MacArthur, the American commander, felt hemmed in by civilian authority. He thought that the military "unleashed" could gain significant victories in Asia. President Truman, on the other hand, feared that it was unwise to involve the United States in a war in Asia. He argued that it was best to limit our objectives and avoid an all-out war with China. The conflict between the military and the government continued to be a problem in the Vietnam war of the sixties, and may well plague any future war the United States may enter.

The Massive-Deterrence Policy

As a result of the Communist threat, other significant changes were likewise taking place in the American military. The pre-World War II concept of rapid mobilization and preparedness to meet aggression and national emergency was reevaluated. In its place, a policy of "massive deterrence" was adopted. In order to stop Communist advance, many thought that the United States would have to be stronger than any other nation. It would have to be obviously prepared to impose heavy destruction on any enemy, so that the enemy would think twice before starting a war. Many began speaking of a "two-and-one-half-war theory," whereby the country would have to be prepared to fight a major war in Europe, a major war in Asia, and a minor war in Africa or Latin America. Achieving such preparedness would require enormous expenditures on the part of the military, and, indeed, soon after the outbreak of the Korean War, those expenditures began to be made.

It was decided that the United States would maintain a modern arsenal of weapons and ammunition, including nuclear weapons. This arsenal would have to be larger than any ever kept by the United States in time of peace. It would mean that the country would have to maintain a level of preparedness unknown in previous military history. Since aggression by the enemy could come at any time, anywhere in the world, the American military would have to be prepared to act with great speed and efficiency.

Foreign policy also began to reflect the belief in the need for strength and massive deterrence. Under President Truman, the United States gave large amounts of aid to Greece, Iran, and other countries in their struggle against Communism. Under Truman, the United States also began to establish a network of treaties and other agreements, so that the nations of the non-Communist world could act in concert against Communist expansion. The Rio Pact with Latin American countries was signed in 1947. In 1949, the cornerstone of American defense policy, the North Atlantic Treaty Organization (NATO), was created. NATO brought together the United States and Canada, as well as ten European countries, in an alliance against aggression. By the terms of the treaty, an attack against one nation was to be considered an attack against them all. Three more European nations later joined the organization. NATO was followed in 1951 by ANZUS, made up of Australia, New Zealand, and the United States. Then, under the new administration of President Eisenhower, these treaties were strengthened and added to by the Southeast Asia Treaty Organization (SEATO) in 1954, the Central Treaty Organization (CENTO) of the Middle East in 1959, and by bilateral agreements with the Philippines, Japan, South Korea, and the Republic of China (Taiwan). John Foster Dulles, Eisenhower's Secretary of State, spoke of a "dynamic foreign policy," and traveled more than any other man who had ever held his office in order to secure this network of treaties against the Communists. The United States had become more deeply involved in the affairs of foreign nations than it ever had before. American military installations were now established throughout the world.

Even though he was later to warn against the evils of the military-industrial complex, President Eisenhower rapidly expanded military expenditure. His administration concentrated on air power above all else and tended to neglect the other services. Massive deterrence and retaliation, it was thought, required faster bombers and rockets. Charles E. Wilson, the Secretary of Defense, said the policy would provide "a bigger bang for a buck." The administration dubbed the policy the "New Look," meaning simply that the United States could not afford to engage the Communists in any number of limited wars. "We can't afford to fight limited wars," Wilson said. "We can only afford to fight a big war, and if there is one, that is the kind it will be." Accordingly, military spending increased rapidly. In 1950 it had been just under $10 billion; by 1956 it had risen to $35.693 billion.

A book published in 1957, however, changed the opinions of many military analysts. The book, *Nuclear Weapons and Foreign Policy*, was written by Dr. Henry Kissinger, who had been chairman of a committee set up to study the policy of "massive retaliation." Dr. Kissinger's central point was that the United States must retain its ability to retaliate with an all-out nuclear attack if sufficiently provoked, but at the same time, it must be prepared to fight in a more limited way against limited enemy attacks. To achieve such a purpose, he felt, the United States would have to maintain an arsenal of weapons and equipment of lesser power, as well as its supply of potent atomic weapons. He also put forth the notion of smaller atomic weapons, atomic bombs that were less powerful than the ones dropped on Japan and which would inflict limited damage.

By the end of the Eisenhower Administration, the Department of Defense had begun to think in terms of a capability for limited conflict as well as full-scale war. But it was left to the Kennedy and Johnson Administrations to put the new ideas into effect. The new military policy of the Kennedy years was termed the "flexible response." It meant that the United States would aim toward being able to respond to a variety of provocations in a variety of ways. The Army was no longer to be neglected. Special units would be set up that could respond to guerrilla warfare and terrorism in jungles as well as cities.

Kennedy and his advisers, however, decided against limiting the nuclear arsenal. Robert McNamara, Kennedy's Secretary of Defense, pointed to the reason. At the time he became Secretary, McNamara said, the Soviet Union had only a small arsenal of operational intercontinental ballistic missiles, but it was known that the Soviets did have the technological and industrial capacity to enlarge their arsenal. Therefore, he felt, the United States had to be ready for any contingency, with the result that the military budget in the sixties quickly rose to over $50 billion a year, and the country's nuclear arsenal was expanded. McNamara later admitted that if he and others in power had known what the Soviets' plans were, the United States probably would not have built up such a huge arsenal.

The McNamara Era

The policy of "flexible response" was not the only innovation that came to the military in the Kennedy years. Important changes affected the whole Department of Defense. The new Secretary of Defense, Robert McNamara, was an innovator. He had been president of Ford Motor Company, where he had made a reputation for himself as an administrator. When he first came to the Pentagon, McNamara was shocked. "This place is a jungle—a jungle," he said. He found the sprawling bureaucracy disorganized. He distrusted the expertise and advice of the Joint Chiefs. He found much quarreling among the three services. No private industry could be run like the Department of Defense and survive, he must have thought. But here was the nation's defense establishment—disorganized, inefficient, in short, chaotic.

McNamara's reforms concentrated on bringing about greater centralization. He brought in his own advisers so that he would not have to rely on the Joint Chiefs of Staff. He angered the Secretaries of the Army, Navy, and Air Force by avoiding them and seeking information from people further down the chain of command. The Secretary of the Army, Elvis J. Stahr, Jr., resigned in protest, saying, "more and more, the decisions once made by the Service Secretaries and military chiefs, as individuals, are made by the Secretary of Defense and his staff."

Two other moves further strengthened McNamara's position

as Secretary of Defense. First, the Assistant Secretary of Defense for Public Affairs organized his office so that information from each service was always in line with the policies of the Secretary of Defense. When information or ideas from one part of the Pentagon went against accepted policy, it was stopped. In that way, McNamara was making sure that his ideas would predominate. In modern times, when so much depends on the flow of information, the possession of information itself becomes a source of power.

The second way in which McNamara made his position more powerful was by the creation of the Defense Contract Audit Agency in 1964. This agency was established to oversee and improve the auditing of Defense Department contracts. The department gave out billions of dollars in business each year. The duty of the new agency would be to centralize and control the enormous number of contracts. What that "control" amounted to was a policing of Defense Department spending by the Defense Department itself, rather than by an independent government agency. McNamara also brought the policy of "cost effectiveness" to the Pentagon as a means of dealing with the demands of the services. "Cost effectiveness" was an elaborate statistical system for the selection of weapons and strategy. It employed the most sophisticated data-processing equipment, and required a large and expensive civilian force to run it. "Cost effectiveness" was another way to exclude the judgment and advice of high-level field commanders and centralize authority in the office of the Secretary of Defense.

Within five years, McNamara had completed most of his reforms. Close observers of the Pentagon noted that department activities had been changed in several significant ways. First, decisions and policy could be made by those in the higher echelons of the department; pressure from Congress was diminished. Second, the Pentagon now presented a more unified aspect. Dissent from military officers and civilian experts disappeared for the most part—at least from public view. Third, defense contractors were placed under greater control, and, to an extent, private industry became a tool of Pentagon planners. Finally, under McNamara there was a concerted effort to give the public a great deal of information about defense policy and attitudes. But that information did not always prove to be accurate and was at times misrepresented or fabricated.

Problems in the Defense Establishment

Since McNamara's retirement, there has been no comparable reorganization of the Department of Defense. Recently, however, demands for change have come from Congress, where a new generation of legislators have determined to limit the power of the military and put some control on military spending. How effective these new attempts at reform will prove remains to be seen, but there does seem to be a genuine new policy of close public and congressional scrutiny of military matters, and in the past few years it has uncovered a host of problems. It has been discovered, for instance, that for thirty years, waste due to inefficiency, mismanagement, and poor judgment has plagued the defense establishment. Men and women who otherwise support the military and argue its necessity have been exasperated by the Pentagon's seeming inability to "clean up the mess." A significant portion of the American public has come to believe that defense spending is simply a means for the rich to get richer and for big industry to flourish, with little consideration for the true defense needs of the nation.

Costs Beyond Control

The waste and inefficiency have been widely publicized in the press and in numerous books. Much of that waste has been in the form of cost overruns on military projects undertaken by private industry. This began to be a problem during World War II, when the practice of granting "cost plus a fixed fee" contracts, discussed earlier, was initiated. Since the government took all the risks, private industry wasn't forced to run efficient operations, as is necessary when their own funds are at risk. In case after case, weapons, ammunition, and other equipment have cost far more than the original estimates allowed, and these extra costs grow with each year and each new military budget. One former Defense Department official admitted that 90 percent of all material the Pentagon purchased from private industry cost more than the original estimates. And this overrun is not a matter of a few dollars. Frequently, it is five or six times the original cost, amounting to billions of dollars each year. If a private business were run in this way, it would collapse in no time.

One of the most blatant of overruns in United States history concerned the cost of the Navy's deep-sea submarine rescue vessel, which increased from $3 million to $77 million! To make it worse, many questioned whether the Navy needed the vessel at all. They pointed out that there had been only two submarine accidents in the past fifty years that the rescue vessel could really have helped in.

In other cases, the cost of the 800 Mark II electronic brains needed in the F-111 fighter planes rose from $600 million to $2.5 billion. The price of the Minuteman II missile rose from $3 to $7 billion. Often, the Pentagon would abandon a project after enormous sums had been spent, with no workable result. Over $1 billion was spent to build a plane powered by nuclear energy; the project was abandoned as futile. The Air Force's Manned Orbiting Laboratory (MOL) program was brought to an end after a cost of more than $1.3 billion.

One of the most famous cases of cost overrun was the case of the C-5A, a huge plane that was to be used to transport masses of equipment thousands of miles on short notice. It was to be as large as a football field, and able to carry fourteen jet fighters or fifty cars. Lockheed bid low and in 1965 received the right to build the plane for the Pentagon at the cost of $3.37 billion. As late as 1968, Pentagon officials were still claiming that the cost of the C-5A was about the same as had been estimated earlier. But soon other figures leaked out. It was discovered that the total cost of the planes (120 of them) would be $2 billion more than had originally been estimated. But there were other facts even more devastating. The tremendous cost overrun had happened even though Lockheed was producing the airplane in a government-owned factory, a plant the government itself had put a tremendous amount of money into, and which Lockheed was using for its own purposes. Not only had the government supplied the factory, it had also supplied most of the company's working capital.

What such a deal amounted to was a welfare program for industry. The government paid substantial sums of money—billions of dollars—so that private industry could gain a profit, pay its executives, and reward its stockholders with dividends. It is true that many jobs were created for workers, but it is certainly possible that these jobs could have been created at less expense to the taxpayer.

The final cost overrun on the C-5A had been $2 billion. To many in the Pentagon, or industry, that may seem a small sum. Yet it is amazing what $2 billion would pay for. At a salary of $10,000 per year, it would finance an army of 200,000 for one year. It would provide a housing subsidy for 3⅓ million American families for a whole year. It would provide all the money needed for one year for the Agency of International Development, a division of government set up to give nonmilitary aid and advice to developing nations, and it is nearly three times the current budget for law enforcement, even at a time when law enforcement is a national priority.

What is more startling is that officials in the Pentagon and industry know that the cost overruns are going to happen, but do nothing about it. Gordon Rule, who served as a cost expert in the

"IT'S NOT TRUE THAT EVERY MISFIRING COSTS THE TAXPAYERS $10 MILLION, SENATOR. WE OFTEN RECOVER SEVERAL HUNDRED DOLLARS WORTH OF SCRAP METAL."

Navy, told the Senate Subcommittee on Economy in Government that the defense contractors know that the systems they build will cost more than they bid. Rule said the following in his testimony before the committee: "Let me put it this way. I think that one of the things that we have got to stop doing in our contracting is playing games—the government and the contractor. We play games. We know that if we tell the DOD across the river how much something is really going to cost, they may scrub it. And they know that if they tell the Congress how much it is really going to cost, the Congress may scrub it.

"So you start with both sides knowing that it is going to cost more. . . . This is what we do. And this is ridiculous. And this is why we get into trouble. How you knock it off I don't know."

The problem grows even larger when it is realized that many of the systems the government pays for not only cost a tremendous amount of money, but they do not even work once they are produced. Between 1955 and 1970, thirteen important aircraft and missile programs with highly sophisticated electronic systems were produced for the Air Force and the Navy. Of those thirteen, only four could be relied upon to reach a level of performance of 75 percent or more of their specifications. Those four cost the government $5 billion. Five of the thirteen performed poorly and broke down easily. Those five cost the government $13 billion. The four others—after costing $12 billion—were dropped or canceled because they were worthless.

Each of the Armed Forces has spent tremendous sums on missiles that were discarded both before and after deployment. The Army gave up on the Hermes, the Dart, the Loki, and others. The Navy abandoned the Sparrows, the Petrel, and the Eagle, among others. The Air Force abandoned the Snark and the Navaho. Altogether, the military spent some $23 billion on these projects, none of which panned out.

Why the Loose Control?

There are reasons why the Pentagon does not police itself and bring an end to this waste. One of the prime reasons is based on the close connections that exist between industry and the Pentagon. Senator William Proxmire of Wisconsin, one of the most astute critics of the Pentagon, has said that the list of such connections is "limitless." Numerous civilians in the Department of Defense have left profitable careers in industry to work at the Pentagon. They have old friends in business—in the very corporations that profit from military spending.

And the relationship often runs the other way as well. Many former military personnel have lucrative jobs in industry. Often these jobs are the very ones that deal with government contracts and the arrangement of projects. Again, Senator Proxmire has been one of the chief critics of this intimate relationship between industry and the military. The senator discovered that the 100 biggest military contractors in February, 1969, which at the time were enjoying military contracts totaling $26.2 billion, were the employers of 2,124 former high-ranking officers.

All this, however, doesn't necessarily indicate some grand scheme or conspiracy to defraud the American public, but rather, that there has been a growing interest between the military and industry for some time, and that such a relationship has not necessarily been good for the nation. It has meant that the Pentagon has been less than efficient in getting the taxpayers' money's worth in arms and military equipment.

The military often replies to the criticism of waste and inefficiency by saying that when all is said and done, the Department of Defense has managed to turn out the most powerful military machine on earth. They argue that cost overruns and other problems are to be regretted, but that they are a natural part of doing business. The highly sophisticated systems essential to the modern military are expensive and require long research and experimenta-

"Seven thousand dollars? I know where
we can get one for $62,800."

tion. What is important, they say, is that in most cases the United States has gotten valuable equipment for its defense money, and that today the country stands prepared for any eventuality.

Yet even here, there is evidence to the contrary. For many critics of the Pentagon, the *Pueblo* incident of 1968 revealed glaring inadequacies in the nation's defense program. The *Pueblo* was a ship that was seized by North Korea in waters off the Korean peninsula. The captain and crew were taken prisoner and accused of spying for the American government. It took more than a year to secure the release of the crew. But to many, it was amazing that the seizure had happened in the first place. When the incident was investigated, it was shown that the forces that were supposed to come to the aid of the *Pueblo* had failed to respond to its call for help. For a full day after the incident, the United States military was not able to call up the small force that had been needed.

A special House of Representatives Armed Services Subcommittee came to the conclusion that the military had proved unable to respond in an important crisis. Part of the report read, "The reluctant but inescapable conclusion finally reached by the Subcommittee is that because of the vastness of the military structure, with its complex division into multiple layers of command, and the failure of responsible authorities at the seat of Government to either delegate responsibility or in the alternative provide clear and unequivocal guidelines covering policy in emergency situations—our military command structure is now simply unable to meet the emergency criterion outlined and suggested by the President himself." This is a frightening conclusion.

The Arrogance of Power

A final problem of the military is its arrogance. When pride in doing one's job becomes excessive, that pride becomes arrogance, blinding an institution or an individual to faults that need to be corrected, and creating a sense of superiority and self-importance that is dangerous in a democracy, where civilian life remains the ideal. One often-cited incident of such arrogance involved the Secretary of Defense, Robert McNamara. In August, 1965, McNamara appeared before the Senate Appropriations Committee. One of the committee members asked the Secretary, "How many divisions do we now have that are well equipped, ready to go into combat?" McNamara responded that the country had sixteen such divisions, and that all were well equipped and ready for battle. When asked again, he repeated his answer, directly and unequivocally. Yet his answer contradicted two studies that had recently been done and which the committee members knew about. In one study, the Senate Preparedness Committee had discovered the divisions to be only 50 percent ready. In the second study, the Pentagon itself claimed them to be only 70 to 80 percent ready.

When further investigation of McNamara's amazing claims was attempted, the senators found their access to information closed down or thwarted. Documents took three to four months to reach them, and were often stamped Top Secret. No one seemed to know any answers. Not only had the Secretary misrepresented the facts to the committee, but the Pentagon also seemed to be dragging its feet, refusing to submit to the requests of elected officials performing their duty.

There are two other examples of the arrogance of power that should be mentioned. These two cases involve men who were employed by the Defense Department, but who chose to be honest about the corruption, waste, and inefficiency they discovered while working for the department. Both stories reveal the extent to which the Pentagon is willing to go to cover up its own mistakes.

John McGee was a native of Mississippi, who served with distinction in the Navy during the Korean War. After the war he returned to civilian life, but later went back to the Navy as a civilian fuel inspector. He was sent to Thailand, where he was to be the only civilian fuel inspector for the Department of Defense. Very soon McGee discovered that his superiors in Thailand had been misrepresenting American oil supplies. He found that millions of gallons of fuel disappeared and were unaccounted for. He protested that fact to officials in the Department of Defense and was ignored. Finally, he wrote to Senator Proxmire, who initiated an investigation. The General Accounting Office, which performed the investigation, discovered that at least 5.5 million gallons of fuel had been stolen.

For his discovery, however, McGee was not rewarded or commended. Instead, he was denied a promotion that was usually given automatically. He found himself ignored and harassed by superior officers. The Navy finally transferred him to Pensacola, Florida, to serve as a laboratory assistant to test oil samples, an obvious demotion. It was, in fact, the same job he had held years earlier when he first began his career. What the Navy seemed to be saying was that it was not necessarily a good thing to reveal corruption. If McGee had not uncovered the scandal and allowed it to go on, he would have found no problem with advancement.

Another case of military arrogance involved A. Ernest Fitz-Gerald. FitzGerald worked for the Department of Defense. He was a high-level civilian cost analyst in the office of the Secretary of the Air Force. He therefore had special informaton about the cost overruns of military projects, and was called to testify before the Subcommittee on Economy in Government in November of 1968. What FitzGerald did amazed the committee. He told them the simple, direct truth, that the C-5A had run $2 billion over its projected costs. The Senate had been trying to get this information for some time, but had met with resistance from the Air Force. The story that follows reveals what happens to a person who confronts a powerful bureaucracy with the truth.

Three months before he testified, FitzGerald had been told that his job with the Air Force was secure. After his testimony, he was informed that a computer error had been made, and that his job was not secure at all. Next, FitzGerald was removed from his old duties. His associates and friends at the Pentagon no longer spoke to him. Further testimony from FitzGerald revealed other problems and misrepresentations in the Pentagon. The Minuteman II missile, for instance, had cost $7 billion, not the $3 billion that Congress had provided. Also, the Air Force had fed Secretary McNamara false information about the cost of the C-5A, so that even the Secretary himself did not know the truth of the matter. FitzGerald likewise revealed that when an Air Force officer had challenged his superiors about the cost of the C-5A, he had found himself reassigned to Addis Ababa, the capital of Ethiopia, as an air attaché.

A year after FitzGerald's first testimony before the Senate subcommittee, his job was eliminated. The Pentagon claimed that it was an economy move, and FitzGerald's work was no longer needed. The military denied that it had any vendetta against FitzGerald. The Secretary of the Air Force dismissed any charges of wrongdoing against FitzGerald as ridiculous. But it is interesting that the Pentagon hired a man to perform many of the duties that had been assigned to FitzGerald. That man was from a company closely associated with Lockheed, one of the Defense Department's prime contractors—and obviously not a person who would challenge the cost of the C-5A, which Lockheed was building. Subsequent criticism of the appointment, however, led to the man's dismissal.

In the past thirty years, the American military has become one of the world's largest defense establishments. It has been organized in the hope that it can deal swiftly and effectively with any threat faced by the United States. It is now military policy to be able to fight any war, general or limited, that might be thrust upon it. From the days of "massive retaliation," the country has come closer to a policy of "flexible response." But the rapid growth of the military and its enormous size and strength have created problems in the defense establishment that must be worked out. Inefficiency and waste abound. Mismanagement and bad judgment are common, and the military is infected with an arrogance that blinds it to its own faults.

Now, however, we'll look more closely at the work of the U.S. Armed Forces at home and abroad. Only when we see their specific duties will we realize how powerful and pervasive the U.S. military has become.

We can divide the activities of the American military at home into several broad categories. First, of course, is defense. But defense has taken on a broader meaning than protection from foreign attack. But it has been used, to a very limited extend, to help in called on to help in national emergencies, such as floods or hurricanes, and to put down riots in major cities. Next, the military has been responsible for a great deal of construction, such as that of highways, bridges, and buildings. Finally, the military has come to play a significant role in the lives of all Americans through its influence on politics and the economy. In the past thirty years, political and economic life have changed markedly in the United States, and the military has done much to effect those changes.

If defense has been the primary purpose of the American military, it has fulfilled that purpose with great energy and determination. Throughout the United States, the Armed Forces have an impressive array of installations. The Army alone has more than forty major installations, from the White Sands Missile Range in New Mexico to the Aberdeen Proving Ground in Maryland. The Navy and Air Force bases add greatly to that number. There are the Strategic Air Command and the various Intercontinental Ballistic Missile sites, not to mention the shipyards, hospitals, research laboratories, arsenals, and numerous other centers. There is a standing army of more than 1.7 million, as well as the National Guard and reserve units. If attacked, the United States could respond with a kick that would be devastating.

National Emergencies

Fortunately, the tremendous power of the U.S. Armed Forces has not been called into action to defend the country from a direct attack. But it has been used, to a very limited extent, to help in national emergencies. The National Guard has often been called up to help restore order when a hurricane, a flood, or some other natural disaster has rendered an area helpless. In March, 1970, President Nixon activated Army Reserve units to sort mail when a strike by mail carriers in New York had crippled business in the city. Both the Guard and the Reserve are sources of a large work force, available in a matter of hours.

The military has likewise been called on to restore order in situations arising from social and political problems. In September, 1957, President Eisenhower sent Army troops into Little Rock, Arkansas, to settle a dispute over racial integration that had grown into a general crisis. Whites were refusing to allow black children to attend a previously all-white public school. Orval E. Faubus, the governor, had called out the National Guard to side with the whites. The governor was a segregationist, and did not want to carry out the ruling of the United States Supreme Court, which stated that public schools throughout the nation must be integrated. President Eisenhower called on the Army to restore

A COLOURED VIEW OF LAW AND ORDER   ROTHCO

The young negro student James Meredith has had a hard fight to gain admittance to Mississippi University in order to study law.
How shall I otherwise learn how to administer justice?

order and see to it that the black children were permitted to go to school.

In the sixties, the use of the military to restore domestic order became more frequent. In July, 1967, 7,000 Guardsmen were called up to aid Detroit police when racial violence threatened the city. Blacks and others were rioting, looting, burning, and fighting one another in one of the nation's worst uprisings. In October, 1967, Army units were brought to Washington, D.C., where a large demonstration against the war in Vietnam was taking place. Labeled "the March on the Pentagon," the demonstration resulted in little actual damage and posed no threat to the power of the Department of Defense.

Military units were again called to Washington in May of 1971 to preserve order during an antiwar demonstration. The protestors had vowed to disrupt traffic and business in the capital and to create general chaos. The police and the military arrested as many as 12,000, placing them in makeshift compounds. Most were quickly released, but authorities later received much criticism for their handling of the demonstrators, and a court awarded large sums of money to those who had been arrested. In September of the same year, National Guardsmen were called on to help put down a riot at Attica State Prison in New York. The Guardsmen were not used in the fighting, but did assist in the evacuation of wounded prisoners and in giving medical care to those who needed it.

But perhaps the most famous case of this period involving use of the military at home happened at Kent State University in Ohio. In April, 1970, students throughout the country protested the U.S. invasion of Cambodia, an action that widened the Vietnam war. Some students at Kent State who were taking part in the general protest began to harass people in the nearby city of Kent, where there was little sympathy for the protesters. A few students even set fire to the campus ROTC building. The gov-

" Anybody else want peace ? ".

ernor of Ohio, James Rhodes, called on the Ohio National Guard to restore order. When the Guard appeared on campus, the student protest deepened. Many of the Guardsmen felt uneasy. On May 4, the Guard fired into a student demonstration, killing four students and wounding several others. The incident shocked the nation. Eight of the Guardsmen were indicted by a federal grand jury for their role in the Kent State shootings, but the result of their trial, which was followed throughout the nation, was acquittal.

The military has therefore been called on several times to use force in settling disputes that have arisen in the United States. But there has also been a more constructive side to military activity in the country. That role has been performed by the Army Corps of Engineers, which built the Panama Canal, but has been responsible for much more. According to its own official history, those of the Corps of Engineers "led the way in exploring the great West. They were the pathfinders sent out by a determined government at Washington. They guided, surveyed, mapped, and fought nature across the continent. . . . They made surveys for work on the early canals and railroads." They also extended the National Road from Cumberland, Maryland, to the Ohio River and beyond, and made the Ohio, Missouri, and Mississippi rivers safe for navigation.

More recently, the Corps has been instrumental in flood control programs throughout the nation. One such project involves rebuilding waterways to make them safe for travel and other uses, and providing flood control, hydroelectric power, or a way to add to the general water supply of an area. Ecological projects have also been undertaken. Pollution control and the end of beach erosion have been among the Corps' pet projects. Each project, the Corps argues, "is an advantage of outstanding importance to national defense."

In recent years, however, the Corps of Engineers has experienced some criticism. Environmentalists argue that many projects the Corps undertakes are unnecessary and often harm the environment they were supposed to improve. When he learned that the Corps was planning to dam the St. Croix River in his home state, Senator Gaylord Nelson of Wisconsin was irate. He knew that the St. Croix was one of the few truly wild rivers left in America, and he saw no reason to destroy it. Nelson compared the Corps to a beaver: "The Corps of Engineers is like that marvelous little creature, the beaver," he said, "whose instinct tells him every fall to build a dam wherever he finds a trickle of water.

But at least he has a purpose—to store up some food underwater and create a livable habitat for a long winter. Like the Corps, this little animal frequently builds dams he doesn't need, but at least he doesn't ask the taxpayers to foot the bill."

Political Influence

One of the ways the military has changed the face of the nation over the past thirty years has been through politics. As the military became wealthier and more powerful, its stake in Congress and other political bodies likewise grew and expanded. Now, the Department of Defense has over three hundred people who serve as lobbyists in Washington. A lobbyist is someone who tries to influence legislation for a special cause. Normally, the lobbyist is nongovernmental, and represents some private interest. This person is paid to visit senators, representatives, and others in power to convince them that certain things need to be done. The Department of Defense has more lobbyists than any other group in Washington. It also spends more money on lobbying than any other lobbying agency, more than the large corporations or banking interests, more than churches or other benevolent organizations.

It is a standard joke in Washington that every time Congress considers a military bill, the military lobbyist, called legislative liaison officers in military parlance, begin to work hard. Reports about America's weakness are given out. The Army announces that the Soviet Union has new weapons that the United States does not have. The Navy warns that the Russian fleet has become far superior to the U.S. fleet. The Air Force declares that it must have a whole new series of airplanes or helicopters. These reports, many observers believe, are made to convince Congress that the military should have all the money it asks for.

Large numbers of well-informed officers testify before congressional committees. Each of these officers carries the same story—

such and such expenditure is necessary if the United States is to maintain its lead in the world. The military lobbyists maintain offices to keep members of Congress informed about military affairs and to urge congressional action on certain bills. These lobbyists answer hundreds of questions every week from members of Congress. On many occasions, they have provided military transportation for senators and representatives on official tours. They provide trips to new installations to show off equipment and new programs. Any congressional legislation concerned with the military interests the lobbyists—bills on retirement benefits, pay, housing, money for new weapons systems, and so on. The exact power of the military lobbyists—the legislative liaison officers—is impossible to measure.

The military can gain power over Congress in another way—through "the pork barrel." The pork barrel is a term used in Washington to describe the use of money to gain favors. Because the Defense Department controls so much money, it can exert a great deal of influence. It can choose to reward a representative with a new military installation in his or her district, thereby bringing more jobs and money to the area. Or the Pentagon can cut off aid to a certain district, thereby causing jobs to disappear. Needless to say, such activity could poison the democratic system by making elected representatives favor any military bill that would bring more money to their districts. The military found its closest friends and supporters in the South, where reelection term after term gave Southern representatives and senators seniority in congressional committees. People like L. Mendel Rivers in the House of Representatives and Richard Russell in the Senate headed important committees that oversaw military budgets and spending, and both men were generally sympathetic to Defense Department demands. It was not an accident that Rivers' district, Charleston, South Carolina, and Russell's native Georgia were greatly rewarded with military contracts and installations. Through

use of the pork barrel both men enriched their constituencies and made themselves popular with the voters.

The Pentagon has other ways of affecting the politics of the United States. One of the most potent methods is speech making. High-ranking officers are respected figures. When they give after-dinner talks, many listen under the assumption that they are people "in the know," whose opinions count. Since World War II, many generals and other important officers have made an enormous number of speeches at countless occasions. They have spoken on military policy and foreign affairs. They have made the Pentagon position on many issues clear and unmistakable. Vice Admiral Hyman Rickover, for instance, made headline news in the late fifties and early sixties for his severe criticism of the American public school system and institutions of higher learning. The Russians had just launched the first artificial satellite, and the United States suddenly appeared far behind the Soviet Union in scientific and engineering capability. Rickover blamed that on education in the United States, which, he said, was inadequate and failed to provide the background necessary for difficult work in science and mathematics.

While Rickover argued that higher learning in the United States suffered by comparison with that of other countries, others believed it had been corrupted by undue governmental influence. As noted earlier, enormous sums were granted important universities to undertake military research. Dr. Nathan M. Pusey, the president of Harvard University, wrote, "No more significant change has occurred in the world of higher education in recent times." And the government that gave so freely of its money could also establish guidelines and rules on how that money was to be spent. It would want to control research and keep close watch on the universities. In the United States, the universities have traditionally been free from government intrusion. They have not taught government doctrine, as in Nazi Germany or the Soviet Union. Would that traditional separation come to an end as a result of government spending? Many feared it would. At Johns Hopkins University, a close relationship between professors and the government came to an end when the professors began to believe that the government was making too many demands. Similar flare-ups were experienced at Harvard, Princeton, and the University of Chicago.

The power of the military also affects the power of the Presidency. Often, the ability of the President to control the budget and lower expenditure is undermined by those in Congress who are sympathetic to Defense Department demands. The President may want to cut defense spending, only to have his views disregarded by representatives and senators whose eyes are on the pork barrel. They know that larger defense budgets mean increased federal spending in their districts and states, which, in turn, means more jobs and a happier constituency.

But the power of the military over the Presidency is not limited to the military's influence over Congress. On three different occasions in the past thirty years, the President has had to muzzle the Department of Defense because some of its officials were directing what amounted to an attack on the Chief Executive and his policies. In 1951, President Truman reminded the Pentagon that he was President and that all releases on foreign policy and military matters should be made only after they had been approved by the civilian officers of the departments of Defense and State. In 1962, President Kennedy reminded the Pentagon of Truman's orders and asked that no partisan statements come from the military that might undermine the policies and authority of the President. And in 1975, President Gerald Ford fired his Secretary of Defense, James Schlesinger, because of their basic differences of personality and opinion on the nation's foreign policy. Schlesinger, a hard-liner on Communism, thought the President had gone too far in détente, or relaxing our relationship, with the Soviet Union.

President Ford, on the other hand, valued détente, and wanted people of like mind in his cabinet.

Economic Influence

If it is true that the military has affected American politics, it is equally true that it has exerted extraordinary influence on the nation's economy. Secretary McNamara made that clear when he said, "We are aware that the award of new defense contracts and the establishment of new defense facilities in a particular area can make the difference between prosperity and depression." The efforts made to land defense contracts on the part of many industries is frantic; often the survival of a company depends on getting a contract.

The importance of defense spending in modern American life is exemplified by the case of Denver, Colorado. The economy of the Denver area expanded tremendously once military spending hit the district. The Martin Company, which subcontracts the Sprint Missile and other military items, is Denver's largest single industry. It does all its business with the government, employing many thousands of people and paying them relatively high salaries. But the influence of the Martin Company does not end there. It provides untold benefits for Denver. By bringing its factories to Denver, the company created new businesses, new shops, and a demand for more housing and new schools. Similar situations occurred all across the country. Prosperity came to Marietta, Georgia, when the Lockheed "Air Force Plant Number 6" was located there. In Eau Claire, Wisconsin, the Northwestern Motors Company saw its total volume of business rise from $1.5 million to $3 million in only eighteen months for the same reason—military contracts. Of course the people of Eau Claire prospered along with the business.

There can be no doubt, then, of the close connection between business and the military in the United States. In Chapters One and Four, we saw that that situation and all the ways it manifests itself in the politics and economics of the country has come to be known as the military-industrial complex. In this complex, business and government spending are so closely related that one cannot do without the other. On the one hand, the government depends on business for a large source of tax revenue to finance the federal budget. On the other, business relies on government to buy military equipment and hardware.

If the government should cut back on its budget, many important corporations would suffer, the economy might collapse, and the prosperity that has characterized American life for two decades could come to an end. Many believe that the American standard of living depends so heavily on the military that we have become a state where disarmament is unthinkable, at least in the near future, because it would ruin the economy.

There is another way in which the military-industrial complex has affected American business. Ten percent of the gross national product is spent each year on arms and military technology. Because this sum is so large, it causes an unhealthy concentration of effort in one isolated segment of the economy. When concentration is on military technology, other productivity suffers. That problem was noted by Senator Hubert Humphrey in August, 1962. Humphrey was impressed by the growth and vitality of the civilian part of several European economies. He spoke of the modernization of factories and products there, while American factories tended to be less innovative and more focused on defense-related production. Humphrey went on to ask, "What is happening to our civilian economy as we plow more and more of our scientific personnel, our brains, into atomic energy for military purposes? Where are we going to end up in this trade competition with these Belgians and these Dutch, who are clever, who are spending more money for civilian aspects and will develop products cheaper, better and more serviceable?" Because the United States paid so much attention to the military, many thought that the country had become second-rate in other fields.

The American military has set up an intricate defense system. It has helped settle riots and other domestic disturbances. It has built bridges and dams. It has entered politics, the universities, and the economy. But there are yet two other ways that it has affected the lives of Americans. One has been constructive; the other, destructive. On the one hand, the military itself has provided education and training for large numbers of men and women. On the other, it has denied basic American liberties to thousands of citizens by spying on them and calling their patriotism into question.

Education and training have been among the basic goals of the American military since World War II. No other country has so comprehensive a system of schools and training centers that offers as wide a selection of programs and fields. Each year since World War II, thousands of young men and women have volunteered for service in the Army, Navy, or Air Force. Some do so because of a feeling of love and responsibility for their nation. Others are attracted by the education programs. They want to learn mechanics or electronics or some other field, and feel, rightly, that the Armed Forces can offer excellent training in those areas. Many young people decide to remain in the military and make it a career; the salaries are good, especially as one rises in the officer corps. Retirement plans and other benefits are excellent.

The Draft

During the fifties and sixties, however, the Armed Forces did not rely on volunteers to fulfill their ranks. For a long time, the Selective Service System was used to get the number of men needed for the national defense. When a young man turned eighteen, he was required to register with his local draft board. He received a Selective Service Card, often called a "beer card,"

"A VOLUNTEER ARMY? WHERE WILL THAT LEAVE US?"

because it provided proof that he was eighteen and eligible to buy beer in many states. If he were a student, he would receive a deferment. He could also receive deferments for other reasons. Some young men who were deferred worked in agriculture or other vocations essential to the national well-being. Others claimed special "hardship" deferments, in which case they had to prove that someone who was unable to work depended on them for income and support. If he qualified for no deferment, chances were that the young man would eventually be called for his "physical." This was a test to see if he were physically, emotionally, and mentally able for military service. If he passed the test, he would be drafted. Many felt the system was extremely unfair, since it took first of all young men who did not go to college. Those who could afford to go to college or who won scholarships were not drafted. Often the college students avoided the draft entirely, taking advantage of other deferments and loopholes in the system.

Now, however, the Selective Service System has been drastically altered. Young men must still register with their draft boards when they reach eighteen, but they will not be drafted. Instead, the Armed Forces rely on an all-volunteer system, using a sophisticated advertising program to attract young people into the service. The "new Army" paints itself in a new image and tries to convince potential volunteers that it offers an attractive career and sound education benefits. Salaries have been raised, and other benefits and conditions improved. The possibilities for education, travel, training, and advancement have become central to the appeal of the Armed Forces, and play an even more significant role than they did under the draft.

But we mentioned earlier that there is a destructive side of the military as well. A few years ago, a Senate committee headed by Senator Sam J. Ervin, Jr., of North Carolina uncovered a vast program of spying and surveillance of private citizens by the mili-

tary. Ervin found such a practice unconstitutional—a threat to the very liberties that the Armed Forces are supposed to defend. The senator argued that the military had no right to spy on private citizens and that by so doing had called into question the honor of many honorable men and women. Anyone suspected of being an enemy of the American military was investigated, from radicals of the far left to nonviolent pacifists, from those who opposed the war in Vietnam to representatives and senators less than friendly to increased military spending. Rumor and hearsay were frequently the basis for investigation, and no effort was made to sort fact from fiction. Ervin reminded the military that it was the servant of the people, not its ruler, and that, like every other branch of government, must act under the Constitution. The Department of Defense promised to put an end to its spying and destroy the files and data that had been collected. Yet indications were that the military was dragging its feet. The files remained and could be put into use.

The American military, therefore, has the potential for both beneficial and harmful effects on U.S. society. This should not be surprising in a body so large and powerful, but it is important that we recognize the potential for harm, and check it before it becomes excessive.

A hundred years ago, it was said that the sun never set on the British Empire. The British had colonies and possessions throughout the world, and at any given time you could be certain that somewhere in the British Empire it was daytime. Today, the same thing can be said of the United States military, with its bases in all parts of the world, with ships constantly at sea and planes always in the air. Some have called the era we live in Pax Americana, the American Peace, just as the world peace maintained by the Roman Empire in ancient times was called Pax Romana. Others, perhaps more critical, have said that the United States has become "the police force of the world."

The United States has some 429 major bases and 2,972 minor bases located in over 30 countries. American military personnel are stationed in Europe, particularly West Germany, in Great Britain, Japan, Taiwan, the Philippines, and elsewhere; altogether, over 600,000 Americans in uniform live abroad, many with their

"THERE'S NO HARM IN ASKING THEM. AFTER ALL, WE'VE BEEN ALLOWED TO SET UP MILITARY BASES EVERYWHERE ELSE."

families. Since the average annual cost of these bases is several billion dollars, many countries find them a valuable source of income and U.S. dollars. Also, the American installations employ over 200,000 foreigners, creating a sizable job market. Just as military spending in the United States helped to bring prosperity to various regions at home, so has the large expenditures of the U.S. military abroad helped improve foreign economies.

After World War II

The deep involvement of the United States in foreign lands came about in two ways. First, American troops occupied the defeated nations of World War II, Japan, and Germany. Order had to be restored to these and the other countries that had been devastated by the war. Since the United States had emerged from the war both strong and prosperous, it was natural that the American military should help restore that order. Next, as was seen in Chapter Three, the threat of the Soviet Union and Communist expansion forced the United States to rearm and seek a worldwide network of treaties and bases to counteract Communist aggression. After World War II, the United States was never able to take any steps toward the isolation from world affairs that it had sought after World War I.

After World War II, Germany was divided among the victorious Allies into four parts. France, Great Britain, and the United States took sections in western Germany. The Soviet Union took the eastern sector. The capital city, Berlin, was itself divided into four parts, but it was agreed that the four sectors would eventually be reunited. Military governors were set up in each of the four divisions of the defeated country. General Lucius Clay was appointed governor of the American region, and took his orders from the War Department, not the State Department. But Clay was an innovative leader in his own right. He encouraged the formation of political parties; indeed, he hoped that elections could take place even before Washington wanted them.

By 1948, it had become clear that the Soviet Union was not going to leave its zone of Berlin as it had previously agreed to do. It even attempted to close off access to any part of the city, which lay within its territory of Germany. Clay was influential in getting U.S. troops and air strength to operate the massive airlift that brought supplies to the city until, eventually, the Communists agreed to let it remain a "free city." France, Great Britain, and the United States decided to merge their sectors into one West German nation, and allow it to function independently. The North Atlantic Treaty Organization (NATO) also emerged from the Berlin Crisis. By this treaty, ten European nations along with Canada and the United States agreed that an attack on one of them would be interpreted as an attack on all of them. American troops remained in Europe to help keep the peace. In Germany, their influence has been particularly strong. Many U.S. military personnel brought their families to Germany; other Americans found German spouses. To this day, troops continue to be stationed there, and the Germans have become America's chief ally in Western Europe, if not the whole world.

The occupation of Japan proceeded differently. The United States had been the principal victor in the war against Japan, and so alone took on the duties of occupation. General Douglas MacArthur was appointed by President Truman to be the military governor. Soon, the general made a reputation for himself as something of a dictator. Japanese officials learned that they had to have his personal approval before they could act. Yet if MacArthur's rule was dictatorial, it was also beneficial. The Japanese were given a new democratic constitution. A land-reform program was undertaken. Education was reorganized. Labor unions were established. New civil freedoms were extended to all people, and laws were passed providing for the equality of the sexes. Troops are still stationed in Japan, but the nation is no longer controlled by the American military. Japan has become an important ally in the Far East. The occupation of Japan and Germany helped establish a tradition of American military aid and assistance—a tradition that grew and expanded in the fifties and sixties.

Communist activity quickly drew the American military into many foreign nations. In 1948, World War II bases in England were reconstructed, this time to handle nuclear bombers. The United States now wanted to be ready, at a moment's notice, to handle any problem like the Berlin Crisis that might arise. In Newfoundland, Iceland, North Africa, the Azores, Spain, Okinawa, and elsewhere, airports, Army bases, and Naval ports were established. These installations have suffered some setbacks in recent years. American forces were asked to leave Libya after the old conservative monarchy there was overthrown by a group of radical young army officers. At the present time, the future of the American base in the Azores and that of the several installations in Turkey seem in doubt, as does the American presence in Thailand and the Philippines. And even the great treaty organizations, such as NATO in Europe, are unsteady and their futures uncertain. But if the American military seems to be leaving certain parts of the world, it is expanding in other parts. Recently, plans were made to establish an island base in the Indian Ocean to offset the strength of the Russian fleet there.

On several occasions in the past three decades, the United States has felt called upon to bring its military into use. The Berlin Airlift and the Korean War have already been mentioned, but there have been other occasions. In 1956, the U.S. fleet in the Mediterranean rescued Americans in the Suez Canal area when fighting broke out between Egypt and Great Britain over ownership of the canal. In 1957, the fleet was again in the Middle East to lend support to the King of Jordan in his attempt to prevent the collapse of his government. In 1958, once again in the Middle

East, Navy, Marine, and Army units lent support to the President of Lebanon, Camille Chamoun, who feared that his government would fall to Moslem rebels.

The early sixties found the military active in other parts of the world. In 1960, a Navy patrol toured the Caribbean to show support for the governments of Guatemala and Nicaragua. Two years later, troops landed in Thailand, in Southeast Asia, on an excursion designed to warn Communist forces in the area that the United States would not tolerate an invasion of Laos, a small country that borders on Thailand. But the most serious crisis of the early sixties occurred in Cuba, where the government under Fidel Castro had moved into the Communist camp. Later it was discovered that the Soviet Union was building missile bases there that could launch nuclear warheads against the United States, only ninety miles away. Most of the major cities and military installations of the eastern part of the country appeared threatened. President Kennedy acted quickly and asked the Russians to leave. He ordered an air and sea blockade of the island, preventing any Soviet ship from reaching Cuba, and keeping out the materials needed to complete the installations. Many feared that Kennedy's action would bring on World War III, but the military blockade proved effective. The Soviet ships decided not to break through, and the missile bases were dismantled. The Cuban Crisis seemed to prove that the U.S. military could move quickly and effectively to protect American interests.

A second Caribbean crisis broke out in the spring of 1965. For several years, the government of the Dominican Republic had been unsettled. Many Dominicans supported Juan Bosch, a poet and leftist, who had been the first fairly elected president of the republic in thirty-eight years when he took office in 1962. His government was toppled by a military regime that had close connections with the United States. By 1965, the situation had become tense, and war had broken out between the left and right.

President Johnson ordered the Marines into the Republic to protect American lives, property, and investments. At first, a force of only 405 was sent, but soon these men were joined by many others, bringing the total to 24,000.

President Johnson claimed that the large force was needed to prevent a Communist takeover. He announced that the United States had information that proved the rebellion in the Dominican Republic had "moved into the hands of a band of Communist conspirators." The United States, he added, would not tolerate another Communist nation in this hemisphere. Many people, however, were skeptical. Throughout the world, the United States was criticized for its action, and the critics in Latin America were among the most vociferous. The administration soon backed away from its claims of Communist subversion and worked out a compromise that permitted Juan Bosch to become part of a new government. But this act only added to the confusion: if the supporters of Bosch were Communist, why was their leader permitted to enter the new government?

The United States had not come out of the Dominican Crisis with its hands clean. For many, it was evidence that the U.S. government was willing to lie to the American public and the world if it suited its interests. It was an early example of a "credibility gap" that would grow to great proportions in the future. The military too was partly held in contempt, for it had been the invader, and the rightist opponents of Bosch were known to have good friends in the Pentagon. Critics of the Department of Defense saw the Dominican invasion as proof of their contention that the United States had become arrogant and militaristic.

Military Aid

American military involvement in world affairs, however, was not limited to U.S. bases abroad and the deployment of American troops in time of emergency. Very early it was believed that the United States would have to help foreign nations beef up their own armed forces so that they could defend themselves. If the rest of the world were strong, then the United States would not have to rely heavily on its own strength, effort, and money. Since World War II, the United States has given enormous sums of money, weapons, and ammunition, as well as training and education, to the armies, navies, and air forces of foreign nations. In the first thirteen years of the program (1950–63) more than $32 billion was spent in sixty-nine different countries. Such aid has declined in recent years, but it still plays an important role in American military policy.

Critics of the program argue that aid has been given indiscriminately. Often it has gone to dictators to help prop up their regimes. It went to one Communist nation—Yugoslavia. Several times it has gone to nations that are traditionally enemies of one another, such as Israel and Jordan, Turkey and Greece. The Department of Defense argues, however, that the program is essential to American security, that the countries involved have benefited for the most part, and that the United States has gotten what it wanted. The seven years of aid to Yugoslavia, for instance, offered between 1950 and 1957, helped to strengthen Tito's stand against Stalin and the Soviet Union, and made Tito friendlier to the United States. The aid to Jordan was necessary because it gave the United States an ally in the Arab world, which had been rapidly withdrawing its friendship because of U.S. support of Israel. The aid to Greece and Turkey was essential because both nations were members of NATO, the cornerstone of the U.S. alliance in Europe. Likewise, both nations were strategically situated—Greece in the Mediterranean, where an important American fleet was located, and Turkey next to the Soviet Union and in control of the entrance to the Black Sea. The friendship of both nations was of paramount importance.

The training given foreign pilots and other military personnel has also helped spread American influence and prestige. Many thousands of young people have come to the United States, often for long periods of time, to learn new military techniques and the handling of modern weaponry and machines. Many foreigners have graduated from United States military academies. A special program to train young African soldiers chosen by their governments was begun in the early sixties. The official handbook on the military-assistance training program describes the advantages of the education policy: "As a side effect trainees from underdeveloped countries obtain a better appreciation of Western culture. Mutual understanding and communication are enhanced by English language training." Studies show that the foreign military personnel trained by American teachers in the United States remain friends of the United States.

The importance of this program can be seen in the following two stories. The first concerns a visit made by General Maxwell Taylor to Iran. In Iran, he witnessed a military demonstration and recorded his reactions. "Last month, I stood on a hilltop in Iran and with some military representatives of the CENTO Alliance watched with the Shah a military demonstration presented by the Iranian Army and Air Force. The explanation to the assembled international audience was made in English by Iranian officers in uniforms similar to the United States field uniform and the briefing bore the unmistakable mark of Fort Benning or Fort Sill. One senses the influence of the American soldier in his role as teacher of the armies of freedom."

The second story comes from Peru. In Peru, a group of young officers overthrew the established government and set up their own. At first, the United States opposed the move. But on investigation of the officers who had seized power, it was discovered that many had received military training in the United States. The man who captured the presidential palace during the coup had been trained at the Ranger School in Fort Benning, Georgia. Another officer prominent among the rebels had recently graduated from the U.S. Naval Academy in Annapolis. Many of the remaining officers had been trained at the American Training School in the Panama Canal Zone. Even much of the equipment they had used had been given Peru through military aid. These facts eventually made recognition of the new government easier.

Military assistance to underdeveloped nations also includes civilian programs that have little to do with weapons or the training of soldiers. President Kennedy recognized the ability of the modern military for constructive work when he pointed out in the early sixties, "The new generation of military leaders has shown an increasing awareness that armies can not only defend their countries—they can help build them." The earliest example of such a program took place in Korea not long after the end of the Korean War. General Maxwell Taylor found that over $15 million worth of construction material was left over. The material had been sent for use in the war, but Taylor thought it could be used by the Koreans to help reconstruct their nation. President Eisenhower agreed that it was a good idea. The project came to be called Armed Forces Assistance to Korea (AFAK). Within the next ten years, nearly five thousand useful projects were completed, including two thousand schools, and many churches, hospitals, clinics, orphanages, civic buildings, and bridges.

These programs have come to be known as "military civic action" programs. In many places, they have proved popular and useful. In Thailand, the Border Patrol Police established many schools in remote areas of the country. The Border Patrol Police are supported with U.S. funds. In Ethiopia, the program built schools, drilled wells, and cleared roads, and won the praise of Haile Selassie, the former ruler. In Turkey, it established literacy-training centers. In Guatemala, it aided irrigation projects that the Guatemalan army had undertaken, and assisted with other projects such as water purification. Another center of the military civic action programs was South Vietnam, where the number of programs was large and the commitment deep.

Other, little-known efforts have likewise been made to influence various people of the world. One such effort was carried out by the Navy, using two destroyers and a seaplane tender. This convoy of three ships traveled from Mombasa, Kenya, into the Persian Gulf, and then on to Ceylon. It put into various ports, where the ships' soccer team played local teams. On several occasions, the crew painted local mission hospitals. A similar fleet traveled along the West African Coast. The purpose of such gestures was to win friends for the United States and show foreign nations that the American military is not always used for destruction and warfare.

The Vietnam War

Unhappily, however, no discussion of the role of the American military abroad is complete without reference to Vietnam. That was the largest and most significant venture the Department of Defense has embarked on since World War II. It was also the most disastrous. It revealed the shortcomings of the U.S. military establishment as nothing else had, and it left the American people bitterly divided. Its effects will be felt for years to come.

America "inherited" the situation in Vietnam when the French army was defeated there in 1954. Vietnam had been a French colony and had struggled for many years to free itself from French domination. Ho Chi Minh, the Communist leader of North Vietnam, was a national hero, for he had been a leader in the fight against the French. The United States was placed in the awkward position of opposing free elections in South Vietnam, for fear the South would vote for Ho, and unwisely supported an unpopular government, headed by the Diem family, members of a Catholic minority in a Buddhist country. The Vietnam issue remained a thorn in the side of the United States.

"I SAY WE **SHOULD** PULL OUT NOW, AND GET INTO A WAR THAT'LL GET US A BETTER PRES[S]

In the early sixties, U.S. military advisers were first sent to Vietnam to "help the Vietnamese help themselves." The situation grew worse, however, and the North was bombed in August of 1964. Ten months later the first U.S. troops engaged the Viet Cong in direct fighting, and by the end of 1965, 200,000 American troops were committed. There seemed to be no turning back. A year later the number had risen to 380,000, and a year after that it had become 475,000.

To many, the spectacle of the strongest nation in the world fighting a small and weak nation was appalling. Yet the small nation held its own. In 1968, after U.S. generals had predicted victory, the North Vietnamese and Viet Cong launched a major offensive, called the Tet offensive, and thereby proved that their strength and will to fight had not diminished. The war was costing the United States at least $25 billion a year. Bombs were dropped regularly on North Vietnamese cities. Chemical warfare was used to defoliate vast sections of Vietnamese jungle. Yet the United States could not gain a victory.

From the beginning of the war, there had been people in the United States who opposed it. As the war dragged on, that number grew. Demonstrations against the military became regular occurrences. The Department of Defense became subject to frequent attacks by the press and on the floor of Congress. At times the bitterness was expressed in violence. "Hard hat" supporters of the military beat up students and others who protested the war. Many young men refused service, burned their draft cards, went to prison, or left the country for Canada or Europe.

Stories of American atrocities in Vietnam circulated in the press. At My Lai, an American lieutenant and his subordinates had killed many Vietnamese women, children, and old people. There were rumors that American soldiers shot their own commanding officers in the back rather than follow orders. There were stories of widespread drug use by American troops. Pictures appeared in newspapers of cages and pits where South Vietnam kept political prisoners. All in all, news from South Vietnam became frightening and unwelcome.

By the time the war was finally brought to an end, the major victim, besides the Vietnamese people, was the American military. The Pentagon was attacked from all sides and defended by few. It was easy to find a culprit in the officers who had been so confident of victory just a few years earlier. Why had the military failed to win the war? Enormous sums of money had been spent. American weapons were supposed to be the most sophisticated on earth. American soldiers had been trained in guerrilla warfare. What had gone wrong?

For many, it was obvious that the generals and civilians who ran the Department of Defense had made flagrant errors and had refused to recognize them as such. Next, the military was attacked because of the frequent lies it had told about U.S. involvement in Southeast Asia and about how well the war was going. Why had the public been so consistently deceived? Everywhere there was proof that the truth had been concealed or distorted. Counts of enemy dead had been enlarged to give the appearance of highly successful attacks. For many months, U.S. planes had dropped bombs in neutral Cambodia, but the Department of Defense continually denied that that was so. These and the many other fabrications and falsifications of the war angered many Americans and exasperated many people throughout the world. Many critics came to the same conclusion: to exert control over the military so that another Vietnam could never happen.

But other sections of the government as well are to blame for Vietnam. Presidents as well as generals lied about the war and misrepresented the true situation. Congress regularly voted money for the war, although it could have cut off funds at any time. And it is true that the military was in large part carrying out policies that had been set elsewhere. The debate over guilt and responsibility will go on for some time. What is clear, however, is that some reassessment of the role of the United States in world affairs needs to be made. Likewise, the role of the military in carrying out American policy must be redefined. The nation cannot afford more Vietnams, nor can it afford to have a divided and confused military.

CHAPTER SEVEN
The Future of America's Military

It is impossible to visualize America's future without the military. It has become too large a part of our lives to disappear overnight. The standing army—once so feared—has become an integral part of our society. Only a few people ever really considered the possibility of a nation without an army. For the rest of us, the military is something we have had to learn to live with.

That does not mean, however, that the Department of Defense should not be changed. The Constitution provides that Congress and the President will have total control over national defense. Those at the Pentagon are the servants, not the masters, of the public and the public's elected officials. In previous chapters, we have seen that the Pentagon has several problems, including wastefulness, inefficiency, and arrogance. It has lost the respect of a large segment of the American public. Clearly, the future of the Defense Department depends a great deal on how those problems are solved. One thing is certain: public respect for the military will increase only when the department learns to deal with its mistakes.

Controlling Waste

There are several measures that the Defense Department can take to end the waste, the overruns, and the inefficiency. Agencies must be set up to oversee defense spending. In the field of military contracting, a switch should be made from military to civilian control. Instead of letting the Pentagon decide which companies to grant contracts, an independent civilian agency could take charge. In that way, military personnel who have vested interests in military contracts would not be allowed to handle those arrangements. As it is now, each of the three services decides for itself the contracting it will do. This results in competition among the services and provides the conflict of interest that is the basic flaw of the military-industrial complex—military personnel who work for industry and business people who work for the Pentagon. An independent civilian agency could be staffed by men and women who have no connections with either the military or industry.

Agencies such as the Bureau of the Budget and the Renegotiation Board, which are responsible for keeping an eye on government spending, should be expanded and strengthened so that they have the work force to review the military budget thoroughly. In the past, these agencies have had to ignore much of the Pentagon's budget simply because they were too small to handle so big and complex an investigation. The addition of a few more staffers to the Renegotiation Board, which is responsible for rooting out excess profits that private firms make on defense projects, would save the government many millions of dollars each year.

Since the Pentagon deals with highly sophisticated equipment, it is necessary too that those who understand that equipment serve on the civilian review agency, the Bureau of the Budget, the Renegotiation Board, and on other agencies set up to police the Pentagon. One problem in keeping close tabs on the military in recent times has been that not enough experts are available to advise Congress, the President, and others in power on highly technical problems. The testimony of those associated with the Pentagon has often been the only source of information and expertise. In the future, any branch of government or agency that sets out to investigate the Department of Defense should have its own staff of scientists and engineers.

Another thing that can be done is to see that any party who fails to carry out a contract is penalized. If products are delivered late, there should be a good explanation, or the contractor should be fined. If the contractors do not build weapons or new equipment according to the specifications that were agreed upon, they should be punished. Cost overruns must not be allowed to go unchecked. There must be regular reports of the cost of various projects so that Congress can keep an eye on what is being spent. This is, after all, the way private business is run. We should ask nothing less of the Department of Defense.

It is important that information be open and accessible. If the problems of the Pentagon are to be solved, there must be no misrepresentation, no lies, and no burying of the facts. There should be complete data available on contracting and subcontracting. There should be complete reports on the performance of new weapons and equipment. Did the United States get its money's worth? If not, why not? How much money is being paid a company to finance a new weapons system? To what extent is the government subsidizing private defense-related industries? What officers, at one time stationed in the Pentagon, now work for private industry? What is their role in private industry? Do they handle defense contracts? And so on. All such information is needed if there is to be a significant change in the Pentagon.

Policy Evaluation

There is another level at which the Pentagon must examine itself. There must be a review of military policy. Such a review would help the Pentagon be more flexible and less tied down to policies that are outdated or unsound. For example, is the so-called "two-and-one-half war" policy wise? According to that policy, the United States is supposedly prepared for a major war in Europe, a major land war in Asia, and a smaller war somewhere else. Is such preparedness realistic, or is it stretching U.S. capabilities too far? There must be further review of our situation in Europe. Do we need so many troops and so much equipment there? What can the Europeans do for themselves that we do for them now? Finally, the more than three thousand American installations scattered throughout the world must come under examination. Which ones are essential and which can be scrapped? That, of course, would entail an examination of American foreign policy, beginning with a review by the President and the Department of State. The Pentagon itself must play a secondary role in foreign policy. In the future, foreign policy must be made by the State Department; the duties and responsibilities of the military lie elsewhere.

To a certain extent, however, the desire for change and improvement must come from the Pentagon itself. Policing agencies, boards of review, and strict civilian control can only go so far to correct the problems the military faces. There must be more evidence that the Pentagon sees its own problems clearly and acts to remedy them.

It is true that many believe the Pentagon has been allowed to get too large for its own good, that it is too centralized and without allowance for innovation or alteration. The ideas of lower-ranking and younger officers are lost in the chain of command. Dissent is not permitted, for fear that it would make the military look weak and divided. The large size of the Pentagon and the centralization of power also create bottlenecks in the flow of all Pentagon activities, from the buying of materials to the establishment of overall military policy. This sort of problem should likewise be investigated by civilian review boards, so that the Pentagon can function effectively.

The tendency of a huge bureaucracy is to become stagnant and uncreative. Such a bureaucracy, bogged down by its own weight, is put on the defensive. It strives to protect its own interests and sphere of power. This is what Congress and the American people must be aware of and prevent from happening in the Department of Defense. That department, after all, is in charge of the very important duty of protecting the United States from its enemies.

In recent years, new developments in foreign policy have provided some little hope that a reduction in defense spending and in the size of the military establishment can eventually be made. Strategic Arms Limitation Talks (SALT) have been held between the United States and the Soviet Union. The negotiations are difficult and tedious, but many believe that important agreements can be reached that will reduce armaments and other weapons of war. Likewise, the policy of détente with the Soviet Union and reestablishment of relations with China may lessen world tension and the threat of war. But these are long-term goals—not ones that can be achieved overnight.

In the efforts to balance the power of the military and make it more efficient and less wasteful, there is an important way in which Congress can help. That is by carefully studying the nation's priorities. When the budget is before Congress, the members must ask themselves whether another $2 billion, or whatever, is needed for a new weapons system or new technological device for the Armed Forces. Would that $2 billion be better spent somewhere else—in the Department of Transportation, for instance? Would it be better for the government not to spend the money at all? By limiting the military budget, by refusing to

"IT'S AN ABSOLUTELY FANTASTIC WEAPON AND DETERRENT. THE ONLY TROUBLE IS IT'LL USE UP ALL THE REST OF THE MONEY IN THE COUNTRY."

hand over to the Pentagon a blank check to get whatever they want, Congress can create a new attitude on the part of the military. Officials in the Pentagon will become more careful about spending if they know they will have only so much to spend, and will not get any more.

In the future, technology will continue to advance, and new weapons and ever more sophisticated equipment will be developed. Costs will expand and put more and more pressure on an already overstrained economy. The United States, although enormously wealthy and powerful, will find itself more and more concerned with economy, efficiency, and frugality in government. It is imperative, therefore, that extraordinary care be taken with the military and its budget—the future of our military, our economy, and our national defense requires it.

In conclusion, the Pentagon has several severe problems, but they are not problems that cannot be solved. Waste and inefficiency can be cut down. The quality of military products can be improved. Cost overruns can be brought within acceptable limits. Even the arrogance that seems so much a part of military life and which has gotten the Defense Department into trouble with the public in the past few years can be controlled. It is good that able reporters and members of Congress have kept a close eye on the Pentagon and have not hesitated to make its shortcomings public. This close scrutiny of military affairs has prevented Pentagon arrogance from becoming all-pervasive. That in itself is a vast improvement on closed societies, where no criticism can be made and the public remains ignorant of the true situation. There is no doubt that improvement *can* be made; the only question is whether it *will* be made.

BIBLIOGRAPHY

David, Jay, and Elaine Crane. *The Black Soldier: From the American Revolution to Vietnam*. New York: William Morrow, 1971.*

Davis, Kenneth S., editor. *Arms, Industry and America*. New York: The H. H. Wilson Company, 1971.

Dupuy, Richard Ernest. *The Compact History of the United States Army*. 2d rev. ed. New York: Hawthorn Books, 1973.*

Engeman, Jack. *Annapolis: The Life of a Midshipman*. 2d rev. ed. New York: Lothrop, Lee & Shepard, 1962.*

———. *United States Air Force Academy: The Life of a Cadet*. rev. ed. New York: Lothrop, Lee & Shepard, 1961.*

———. *West Point: The Life of a Cadet*. 2d rev. ed. New York: Lothrop, Lee & Shepard, 1967.*

Fulbright, Senator J. William. *The Pentagon Propaganda Machine*. New York: Liveright Publishing Corp., 1970.

Glines, Carroll V. *The Compact History of the United States Air Force*. 2d rev. ed. New York: Hawthorn Books, 1973.*

Gurney, Gene. *The Pentagon*. New York: Crown Publishers, 1964.*

Hammond, Paul Y. *Organizing for Defense: The American Military Establishment in the Twentieth Century*. Princeton: Princeton University Press, 1961.

Heiman, Grover, and Virginia Heiman Myers. *Careers for Women in Uniform*. Philadelphia: Lippincott, 1971.*

Hicken, Victor. *The American Fighting Man*. New York: Macmillan, 1969.

Just, Ward. *Military Men*. New York: Alfred A. Knopf, 1970.*

Knox, D. W. *A History of the United States Navy.* New York: G. P. Putnam's Sons, 1948.

Marmion, Harry A. *The Case Against A Volunteer Army.* Chicago: Quadrangle Books, 1971.

Pierce, Philip N., and Frank O. Hough. *The Compact History of the United States Marine Corps.* New York: Hawthorn Books, 1964.*

Proxmire, Senator William. *Report from Wasteland: America's Military-Industrial Complex.* New York: Praeger, 1970.*

* Indicates books geared to younger readers.

ABOUT THE AUTHOR

Stephen Goode has been a member of the history faculty at Rutgers University, specializing in European social and intellectual history. He holds degrees from Davidson College, the University of Virginia, and Rutgers.

Mr. Goode, who at present is engaged in research and writing in Washington, D.C., has authored for Franklin Watts two other books on contemporary history and political science: *Affluent Revolutionaries: A Portrait of the New Left* and *The Prophet and the Revolutionary: Arab Socialism in the Modern Middle East.*